Pagan Portals
Gods & Goddesses
of England

Pagan Portals
Gods & Goddesses
of England

Rachel Patterson

**MOON
BOOKS**

Winchester, UK
Washington, USA

JOHN HUNT PUBLISHING

First published by Moon Books, 2023
Moon Books is an imprint of John Hunt Publishing Ltd., No. 3 East Street, Alresford
Hampshire SO24 9EE, UK
office@jhpbooks.net
www.johnhuntpublishing.com
www.moon-books.net

For distributor details and how to order please visit the 'Ordering' section on our website.

ISBN: 978 1 78904 662 5
978 1 78904 663 2 (ebook)
Library of Congress Control Number: 2022936787

A CIP catalogue record for this book is available from the British Library.

Design: Matthew Greenfield

UK: Printed and bound by CPI Group (UK) Ltd, Croydon, CR0 4YY
Printed in North America by CPI GPS partners

We operate a distinctive and ethical publishing philosophy in
all areas of our business, from our global network of authors to
production and worldwide distribution.

Contents

Contents

Introduction

I live in England and have always been fascinated by the gods and goddesses from the land I live on.

My pathway has been a Pagan one for many years. Initially I looked to the Celtic pantheon because it made sense as I lived in the United Kingdom. This had its uses, but I did note the majority of these deities were linked with Ireland, Wales or Scotland, England seemed a bit lacking. Then I opened up to deity as a whole and I ended up working with gods and goddesses from across the globe. But none of them stuck for very long. Until I met The Cailleach, an ancient goddess hailing generally from Scotland. (See my book *Pagan Portals The Cailleach*). I walked beside her for many years and feel truly blessed to have done so. More recently, however, I have felt drawn to focus more on England, not just because I live here but it was a prompt when my son had an ancestry DNA test done. The test revealed he was 75% English and 25% Scandinavian. He also discovered he is a direct descendant of Eric the Red. That was the real push that I needed, down into the rabbit hole leading me on a journey to unearth gods and goddesses from England, those that were worshipped long before the Romans arrived on our shores to set up camp. Echoed by a visit to the royal city of Bath, in Somerset, many years ago now, where I connected with the goddess Sulis (and numerous subsequent visits).

This book is all about them.

I invite you to journey with them and make your own discoveries.

Part I
The History of Humans

The History of Humans

The very short version: Evidence of humans living in Britain has been found to date back to c. 700,000 BCE. However, in 25,000 BCE we were hit by an Ice Age and forced to head southwards to warmer lands. At the end of the Ice Age, we returned and were hunters and fishers. We followed the animals as they moved across the land with the seasons. Eventually we settled and became farmers.

Let's look at the Isles

We need to start with the names of the United Kingdom and Great Britain. Although both are used interchangeably, there is a difference. The British Isles sit off the north western coast of Europe. The main islands are Britain and Ireland, with a few smaller ones. During the Middle Ages Britain also contained Brittany, which is a part of France. Great Britain was the name used to refer to the island. In 1707 England and Scotland were united and became Great Britain. Although Ireland was an English colony it didn't unite under the Great Britain banner until 1801, making it the United Kingdom of Great Britain and Ireland, or United Kingdom to use the shortened version. Then in 1922 Ireland (except for six northern counties) left the union to become a sovereign republic.

To sum that up:

- Great Britain is a geographical name for the island known as Britain covering England, Wales and Scotland.
- United Kingdom of Great Britain and Northern Ireland includes Great Britain and Northern Island.
- Ireland includes the Republic of Ireland and Northern Ireland.
- The British Isles is a term that covers all the above.

Timeline

I think it helps to look at the timeline for Britain, just to put this information into a sensible perspective. This is very brief outline, obviously a lot more went on than I have included here. It really is a fascinating subject if you are interested, and I recommend delving into it in more detail if you can. I have covered from the date the earliest human existence has been discovered through to 1066CE. Obviously, there is a huge historic timeline after that to present day, but for the purpose of the Pagan deities we are looking at, further than that isn't overly relevant.

Palaeolithic Britain

c. 700,000 BCE	–	The earliest human implements found in Britain
c. 130,000 BCE	–	Appearance of the Neanderthals in Britain
c. 30,000 BCE	–	Disappearance of Neanderthals from the archaeological records
c. 12,000 BCE	–	Beginning of the end of the last Ice Age, Britain re-colonised by homo sapiens

Mesolithic and Neolithic Britain

c. 9000 BCE	–	End of the last Ice Age
c. 4200 BCE	–	Farming began to spread throughout Britain and the earliest found long barrows
c. 3000 BCE	–	The end of long barrow construction and the beginning of henges and stone circles
c. 2800 BCE	–	The build of Stonehenge begins
c. 2750 BCE	–	The earliest Beaker burials
c. 2700 BCE	–	The use of copper in Britain begins
c. 2300 BCE	–	The use of bronze in Britain begins

Iron Age Britain

c. 650 BCE	–	Weapons change from bronze to being made with iron

c. 600 BCE	–	The Celtic style long sword comes into fashion in Britain
c. 550 BCE	–	Hillfort construction begins in central southern Britain

The Romans

55 BCE	–	Roman forces land in Britain, in Deal, Kent – and fail to take a hold
54 BCE	–	Roman forces land in Sandwich, Kent
43–47 CE	–	Most of southern Britain is pacified by the Roman Alus Plautius
44–48 CE	–	The hillfort tribes in the south west are subdued
57 CE	–	South Wales succumbs
60–61 CE	–	Queen Boudicca revolts against the Roman army in southern Britain
60–early CE	–	Romans control Britain to the Dumnonii land west of Exeter, Devon
68–70 CE	–	Battle against the Druidic cults, finally defeating them
68–69 CE	–	Roman garrisons are sent over to Europe during the civil war
70 CE	–	Vespasian decides to take on complete domination of Britain
71–73 CE	–	The Brigantes tribe finally defeated by the Romans
74–77 CE	–	The Silures and Ordovices tribes succumb to the Roman governor
78 CE	–	The conquest of Britannia is completed by Julius Agricola
79 CE	–	Agricola takes on the invasion of Scotland
80 CE	–	Roman forts are built at Forth Clyde, Scotland
82 CE	–	The south western Scotland tribes succumb

122 CE	–	Hadrian's Wall was built to separate the 'barbarians and Romans'
150 CE	–	Ptolemy adds Scotland to his Geographia
180 CE	–	Serious raids began into northern Britannia
c. 200 CE	–	The northern tribes come together to create larger groups
208 CE	–	The Romans make a last attempt to conquer Scotland, led by Septimius Severus
210 CE	–	Britannia was divided into two imperial provinces
250–274 CE	–	Civil war and Gothic invasion causing imperial crisis
260–174 CE	–	Britannia become part of the breakaway Gallic empire
c. 280 CE	–	Raids by the Germanic Saxons escalate
286–293	–	Carausius rules the Empire of Britain
c. 290 CE	–	Saxon shore fortifications are built on the east and south coasts
297 CE	–	The existence of Picts is first recorded
306 CE	–	Britannia is divided into four imperial provinces
c. 360 CE	–	Many Roman towns are abandoned
367 CE	–	Britannia is invaded by Saxons, Picts and Scots
369 CE	–	Theodosius brings order back to Britannia
383 CE	–	Magnus Maximus severely weakens the British legions
c. 400 CE	–	Hadrian's Wall is completely abandoned
401 CE	–	Roman legions are sent over to the Italian campaign
407 CE	–	The rest of the Roman legions leave for Gaul

The Germanic Invaders, Picts and Scots

| c. 440 CE | – | Germanic peoples settle in southern Britain |

457 CE	–	Saxons claim victory over the Britons at Crayford, Kent
c. 480 CE	–	The Saxons expanded westward
c. 500 CE	–	The kingdom of the Scots, Dal Riata is formed in Argyll
c. 510 CE	–	Saxons advanced into Hampshire
c. 550 CE	–	The centre of British power focuses around the western counties

The Christian Saints, the Dark Ages, Vikings and Danes

560 CE	–	Saint David (Dewi Sant) established monasteries in Cornwall and Wales
563 CE	–	Columba arrived in western Scotland and an abbey is built on the island of Iona
577 CE	–	The British Cornwall and those of Wales are separated after the defeat at Deorham
597 CE	–	Augustine arrives in England accompanied by forty monks
600 CE	–	A large part of Scotland is under Pictish control
604 CE	–	Union of Bernicia and Deira
616 CE	–	Aethelfrith defeats the Welsh, separating the Welsh from Cumbria
635 CE	–	Aidan starts a mission to the Northumbrians
638 CE	–	Oswald captures Din Eidyn
655 CE	–	Oswiu defeats the Mercians
664 CE	–	Synod of Whitby supports the Roman Church traditions
674 CE	–	Monasteries are built in Northumbria
685 CE	–	the elite of Northumbria are defeated by the Picts
785 CE	–	A border is created between Powys and Mercia by Offa's Dyke
830 CE	–	Much of the land held by the Picts is now

		controlled by the Norse
840 CE	–	The Norse plough deep into Ireland and western Scotland
843 CE	–	The Picts and Scots are united under Kenneth MacAlpin
850 CE	–	Much of Wales is ruled by Rhodri Mawr
850 CE	–	Southern England is invaded by the Danes
865 CE	–	The Great Heathen army of the Danes arrive
878 CE	–	The Danes are defeated at Edington by Alfred
915 CE	–	Edward, son of Alfred restores the Danelaw to English rule
930 CE	–	A border is created along the Tamar between Cornwall and England
942 CE	–	Gwynedd is added to the kingdom of Hywel Dda
950 CE	–	The King of Wessex, Aethelstan reabsorbs most of northern England
991 CE	–	the Danes call victory at Maldon, Essex
991 CE	–	the Danes are bought out by Aethelred for 4500kg of silver
1002 CE	–	The Danish elite are massacred in England (named St Brice's Day)
1013 CE	–	Aethelred of England flees to Normandy
1017 CE	–	Cnut the Great, a Dane becomes king in England
1039 CE	–	Llywelyn's power of Gwynedd is expanded
1040–1057 CE	–	Rule of Macbeth of Alba
1042–1066 CE	–	Edward the Confessor is King of England
1058 CE	–	Malcolm III, becomes King of the Scots

The Normans

1066 CE	–	Harold II (Godwinson) becomes King of England

1066CE   –   York is captured by invading Norwegians
who defeat the earls of Mercia and
Northumbria

In this year the Duke William lands at Pevensey, the Battle of Hastings occurs (originally called Battle of Senlac), William moves towards London and then finally on December 25th he is crowned at Westminster, William I.

Burials

We can learn a lot from how our ancestors buried their dead. Finding these burial sites has helped us understand them. How the dead were buried may have been influenced by travellers arriving from other countries and perhaps our people adapting and changing to new ideas and influences. 4200BCE onwards saw the trend of collective burial. The dead were left to rot and stored safely until they were just bones, these were then transferred to burial chambers. Often these were great earth mounds lined with slabs of stone. These we recognise as 'barrows'. Each barrow contained anywhere between five and fifty bodies, the suggestion being that these people held high status within the group. In the north and west of Britain these burial chambers are stone tombs often referred to as 'dolmens'. The dolmens had separate chambers used for feasts, rituals and then the human remains which were often sorted into age and sex. Some stone chambers or 'passage graves' in North Wales and Ireland held hundreds of remains. More common folk it seems found their resting place left open to the elements and wildlife, ending up in ditches.

A change came about when Beaker burials occurred, somewhere around 2750 BCE. The collective grave system was abandoned in favour of single graves covered with a small mound. The body was placed in a foetal position inside a stone coffin, often with added grave goods such as pottery. Cremation was a favourite in the north of Britain, but about the same time as Beaker burials became popular, cremations also found their way down south.

The Monuments

The British Isles are scattered with ancient monuments, henges and stone circles. A lot of them dating between 3000–2300 BCE. Henges are classed as circular areas which are enclosed by an earth bank and ditch. Remains of humans have been found at a lot of henge sites. It has been recognised that these sites must have had a religious significance.

Metals

Once metal made an appearance in Britain things changed. Copper daggers have been found that date to 2700 BCE, although, it is believed these may have made their way over from Europe. Copper items were beaten into the required shape by stone axes. Followed by more complicated designs once the skill of smelting and casting was perfected. Circa 2300 BCE we started adding tin to the mix and bronze came into being, from which much stronger tools and weapons were made. Copper was found in Wales, Derbyshire and the Isle of Man, and Cornwall provided the tin. Scroll on to 650 BCE and bronze was replaced by iron.

Offerings

We can gain a lot of information from the offerings found in archaeological digs on Roman sites, ancient monuments and even in rivers, wells and fresh springs. If offerings were given of a flora or fauna nature then obviously, they are more difficult to detect because they would decompose. But metal objects, coins, implements, swords, daggers, jewellery and pottery have all been found which tell a story.

Iron Age

Circa 650–100 BCE we mark the Iron Age. The population in Britain was on the rise with the ripple effect of trade and production of goods increasing. The tribal rivalry also increased which spurred building of fortifications.

The Celts

Celtic is a collective name for a whole lot of peoples. Usually applied to those hailing from central to western Europe after 800 BCE. Iron Age Britain held a diverse culture of peoples all who took influence from Celtic Europe through trading and family ties. They also held common Druidic beliefs.

The Druids

During the last few centuries BCE and up to and including the Claudian invasion of Britannia (43 CE) the Druids were the High Priests in charge of religion throughout Britannia and Gaul. Caesar, Pliny and Cicero wrote about the Druids, some factual other information perhaps more fanciful. But it shows how important the Druids were at the time and that they were a force to reckon with against the Romans. The Romans told of cannibalistic acts and ritual human sacrifices, all supposedly carried out by the Druids, most of which I suspect was a huge embellishment of the truth. Whilst archaeological finds from the Iron Age show evidence of religious and cult activities, nothing can definitely be attributed to the Druids.

The Tribes of Ancient Britain

Each tribe in ancient Britian had a specific area with its own monarch. I have shared a brief amount of information here just to give you some perspective on the deities within this book. If you are interested, I do recommend researching further, there are some fascinating books on the subject that I have listed at the end of this book.

My research is drawn from various sources, but obviously we don't know any of the exact details for sure. The ancient Britons were not particularly good at keeping written records. So bad in fact that their written history is pretty much non-existent. What we know about the ancient tribes of Britain comes from the Romans.

In or around 150 CE (I don't remember the exact date, I must have been busy elsewhere), the Greco-Egyptian astronomer, mathematician and geographer, Claudius Ptolemaeus, known to his friends as Ptolemy, created what comes together as a basic map of the world. This map obviously included Britain. Although the shape was somewhat squiffy, he details the tribes. He worked from information created by Marinus of Tyre whose sources date back further to around 100 CE. Most of the details on Britain would, however, have come from the Roman military.

The list is as complete as possible, but with the sketchy records there may be some omissions. Unless you are that old and can remember it personally, I don't think anyone will know. Although this book only covers deities from England, I have included the tribes for Scotland and Wales too.

The tribes are also important because archaeological finds have discovered most of them gave offerings often thrown into bogs, lakes, rivers and natural water springs. Some of the offerings were in the form of jewellery, coins, decorated metal, pieces or armour and other fineries. This shows they were honouring deities or spirits of nature in some way. This seems to have been the general 'birth' of deities in ancient Britain, by way of the people worshipping the local water in some way. I suspect if you lived near a river, it was a force that could give live by way of providing food but also take life by drowning. Definitely something to keep on the good side of.

I present this information here so that you can have a look at the tribe that occupied the area you live in, if you are in Britain. It can help you connect and understand the civilisation as it was when the ancient deities were worshipped. I am hopeful too that it will help you connect with the land beneath your feet.

Northern Scotland, the area above the Forth and Clyde estuaries, was never fully controlled or occupied by Romans. Ptolemy's list includes twelve tribes for this area, most of these tribes are only referenced in Ptolemy's writings.

Cornovii – Ptolemy records this tribe as located in Caithness, the northern part of Scotland.

Caereni – Ptolemy places this tribe on the western coast of Sutherland, Scotland.

Smertae – Ptolemy puts the Smertae in Sutherland, Scotland.

Lugi – Ptolemy puts the Lugi in the area of the western coast of the Moray Firth.

Decantae – Ptolemy lists these on the western coast of the Moray Firth in Cromarty Firth.

Carnonacae – Ptolemy puts this tribe on the western coast of Ross-shire, Scotland.

Creones – Ptolemy puts the Creones on the west coast of Scotland, south of the Isle of Skye and north of the Isle of Mull.

Vacomagi – Ptolemy places the Vacomagi in the north east of Scotland, the Cairngorms. with their centres or main towns as Bannatia, Tamia, Pinnata Castra and Tuesis.

Taexali – Ptolemy puts this tribe on the north east coast of Scotland, the Grampians with a central town of Devana.

Epidii – Ptolemy puts this tribe in the region of Epidion, later identified as Kintyre, Arran, Jura, Islay in Argyll.

Venicones – Ptolemy places this tribe in Orrea, which we now believe to be located in Monifieth in Scotland.

Caledonii – It looks as if the term Caledonii was used as a general term for the whole area. Although the Caledonii tribe was based in the Great Glen area.

Damonii – Central Scotland. Glasgow, Strathclyde, Clyde Valley, Ayrshire.

Novantae – According to Ptolemy this tribe was based in Carrick, Dumfries and Galloway.

Selgovae – Central area (the name means 'hunters') Southern uplands of Scotland. Tweed basin.

Votadini or Otadini – Two different names for what seems to be the same tribe. They covered South east Scotland and North east England, Firth of Forth and down to Northumberland. Their centre was the Traprain Law hill fort in East Lothian, Scotland which moved later to Din Eidyn (Edinburgh).

Brigantes – Brigantes translates as 'high ones'. Referring perhaps to the hills of the Pennines in the area. The area between the Tyne and just into southern Scotland, down to the Humber and Mersey, including the Peak District, Pennines, Yorkshire, Cleveland, Durham, Lancashire, Northumberland and parts of Durham. From the North Sea to the Irish sea. It seems the Brigantes tribe may have included smaller tribes, or 'septs' as they were called, these were: Setantii, Lopocares (based in Corbridge, Northumberland), Corionototae and Tectoverdi. The centre was Isurium Brigantum (Aldborough). The Brigantes had a Queen, Cartimandua. The suggestion is that Stanwick in North Yorkshire was her base. She was a Roman ally. The territory they covered made them the largest tribe in Britain. Their name bears a striking resemblance to the goddess Brigantia and some sources believe this is where it was derived from.

Carvetii – Possible name meaning 'deer men'. Covering what we now know as Cumbria, parts of north Lancashire, south west Durham in England and south east Dumfries and Galloway in Scotland. Their centre was thought to have been at Luguvalium (Carlisle). Ptolemy did not include them in his writings as they may have been part of the Brigantes by then. But their name is mentioned on three inscriptions which include a tombstone and two milestones.

Parisi – Ptolemy notes their town as Petuaria, which may have been located in what is now Brough on the River Humber. He puts them near Opportunum Sinus (sounds like something from a medical dictionary), which is in East Riding in Yorkshire. If the name Parisi looks a little familiar there is a suggestion of links to a tribe in Gaul with the same name. In the Parisi area it seems their burial practices were unique to Britain and parallel to those of the Gaulish tribe.

Demetae – Ptolemy had made a record that the Demetae occupied South west Wales. Pembrokeshire, Carmarthenshire. The county of Dyfed takes its name from this tribe. However, the name of Octapitarum Promontorium was given to the area St David's Head, which would suggest the tribe there was called the Octapitae.

Silures – South east Wales. Brecon Beacons. South Welsh valleys, Glamorgan and Monmouthshire. The capital being

Venta Silurum (Caerwent). There are remains of a number of their hillforts across this area. Silures translates from Latin to mean 'the people of the rocks', which is shown by the mountains they lived in.

Ordovices – South Gwynedd, south Clwyd, North West Wales, parts of western Shropshire and Hereford & Worcester. The Llyn Peninsula, however, was named Ganganorum Promontorium which would lead us to believe it was inhabited by a tribe called the Gangani.

Gangani – There is only one reference to this tribe, by Ptolemy who called the Llyn Peninsula the 'promontory of the Gangani'.

Deceangli – North east Wales, although not mentioned by Ptolemy. Isle of Anglesey/Mona, parts of Flintshire and areas of Cheshire. This tribe lived in hillforts in the area, the centre of which was Canovium (Caerhun).

Setantii – Ptolemy refers to Portus Setantiorum (Port of the Setantii) and places them on the western and southern coast of Lancashire.

Textoverdi – A tribe believed to have lived on the western and southern coastline of Lancashire. There centre was thought to be either at Beltingham or Corbridge.

Cornovii – Staffordshire, Shropshire, Cheshire, the Wirral, north Herefordshire and easter parts of Powys. Two particular towns are mentioned by Ptolemy. Their capital which we know as Viroconium Cornoviorum (Wroxeter), Shropshire and Deva (Chester). Cornovii has been suggested to mean 'people of the horn'. There also seems to be traces of the Cornovii in the south west with the place name Durocornovium which translates as 'fortress of the Cornovii'. The name 'corn' has survived as part of the county name of Cornwall. The 'wall' part of the name coming from Anglo Saxon meaning 'native Britons'. Here perhaps the translation of Cornovii being 'people of the horn' referring to the shape of the peninsula of the coastline. And as mentioned above, there was also one in Caithness, Scotland.

Corieltauvi (Coritani/Coritavi) – According to Ptolemy their main towns were Lincoln and Leicester. East Midlands. Lincolnshire. Leicestershire. Nottinghamshire. Derbyshire. Rutland and Northamptonshire. Ptolemy referred to the tribe as Coritani or Coritavi. More recent discoveries suggest the name was Corieltavi. The capitals were Lindum (Lincoln) and Ratae Corieltauvorum (Leicester).

Dobunni (Bodunni) – Southern Severn Valley, Cotswolds, Mendips and including Gloucestershire, most of Worcestershire, into Oxfordshire, Wiltshire, Bristol, Herefordshire, Warwickshire, Wiltshire, Breconshire and Somerset. The capital was Corinium Dobunnorum (Cirencester).

Catuvellauni – Hertfordshire, Bedfordshire, Southern Cambridgeshire and Buckinghamshire. Parts of Oxfordshire. Northamptonshire, Essex and Greater London. Their capital originally was near Wheathampstead but moved to Verulamium (named by the Romans) which is modern St Albans, Hertfordshire. Their name is thought to come from 'cat' meaning battle and 'vel' meaning leader.

Belgae – Hampshire. Their capital Venta Belgarum is now Winchester. Some records seem to suggest that the southernmost reach of the Dobunni was also covered by the Belgae. Including Aquae Sulis or what we know as Bath in Somerset. It seems the Belgae travelled over to Britain from

Gaul somewhere in the 1ˢᵗ century BCE.

Trinovantes – North of the Thames in the Essex area, Colchester, Suffolk. Trinovantes translates roughly to 'vigorous or very lively'. Originally their centre was Braughing in Hertfordshire, but it was thought to have moved to Camulodunum (Colchester). The Trinovantes helped Boudica in her revolt against the Romans.

Cantiaci/Cantii – Kent, East Kent, East Sussex and Greater London. A Belgic tribe that came over during the 2ⁿᵈ Century BCE. They were made up from smaller kingdoms that could come together when needed. Their centre was Durovernum Cantiacorum which we know as Canterbury, Kent. Sometimes referred to as 'people of the corner land', I assume because of their location.

Atrebates – Along the south coast, Surrey, West Sussex, Hampshire and Berkshire. It seems the Atrebates were a Belgic tribe from Gaul. Somewhere around 30 BCE / 50 BCE (sources differ) their King, Commius migrated over to Britain. Their capital was, Calleva Atrebatum which is modern day Silchester, Hampshire. Later on, they also had a centre at Chichester, Sussex.

Regni/Regnenses/Regini – Their territory seems to overlap with that of the Atrebates, perhaps they were part of a collective. Suggestions are they covered parts of east and west Sussex and parts of Hampshire and Surrey. It seems this tribe may not have existed before the arrival of the Romans. Their capital was Noviomagus Reginorum, or Chichester in West Sussex as we know it today.

Iceni – Norfolk, Suffolk, Lincolnshire and Cambridgeshire. Perhaps the most famous connection to the Iceni tribe is Boudica who led a revolt against the Romans. Their centres were at Snettisham and Thetford.

Durotriges – Dorset, south Wiltshire, south Somerset and Devon east of the river Axe. Perhaps a group of smaller tribes. The suggestion has been made that their main residence was Maiden Castle, a hillfort but Hod Hill and Hengistbury Head have also been put forward. Once the Romans moved on from there, Durnovaria (Dorchester) may have been taken on as the capital of the Durotriges.

Dumnonii – Probably a group of smaller tribes. They seem to have strong connections with their Gaulish neighbours in Brittany. Southern and western Somerset, Cornwall (originally called Cornubia) and Devon. Dyfneint was the original name for Devon which possibly translates to 'deep valley dwellers'. Somerset being the 'summerland' of the Mabinogion. Dumnonii derives from a Gaulish word which means 'the masters' or 'dominators'. Their capital was originally Keresk or Caer Uisc which we know now as Exeter, Devon. The Romans called it Isca Dumnoniorum. The Dumnonii had links with Brittany.

The Romans

Although the Roman's first attempt at invading Britain failed, they did eventually succeed. Not all the tribes were happy about it, some fought bitterly against the invaders. The first to fall were the Catuvellauni tribe. The tribes of Durotriges and Dumnonii were very hostile towards the Romans as were the Silures and Ordovices. The Druids of north Wales and Anglesey in particular held fast for a long time. Queen Boudicca of the Iceni tribe is famous for leading a revolt against the Romans. Boudicca is such a notable figure in Pagan history. The Roman historian describes Boudicca as tall with a *'great mass of tawny hair falling to her hips'*. She apparently wore a golden necklace and a tunic of many colours. Her first act before mounting the revolt against the Romans was to release a hare from the folds of her dress, the path the hare took was a sign of support from the gods and was meant to encourage her warriors to follow her into battle. They were soon joined by other tribes such as the Trinovantes.

The town of Camulodunum (Colchester) fell and the population slaughtered. The fall of Londinium (London) came soon after along with Verulamium (St Albans). It was a massacre. The Romans re grouped and met the Iceni in battle near the town of Towcester. Their discipline and experience brought them victory over the Iceni. The Roman historian Tacitus recorded that Queen Boudicca poisoned herself rather than be taken captive. After this grand event, southern Britain became totally under the control of the Romans. Southern Scotland was lured by the promise of Roman support and modern ideas such as road building. The north of Scotland was not convinced, the tribes there remained hostile. The Forth Clyde valley was a separating point between Britannia and Caledonia. Hadrian's Wall is also a separation point built to prevent small raids. It is literally a wall that stretches 130km/80 miles across the landscape. Although these days huge parts of it have been dismantled or ravaged by weather and time.

The Roman presence in Britain had a profound affect and influenced our landscape and culture greatly. Those areas that had a strong Roman presence began to integrate themselves and the lifestyle of their invaders. Although pre-Roman Britain had some coinage, it was during the Roman occupation that money began to be used on a regular basis. Trade with other countries also grew. And, of course, the faith and beliefs began to merge somewhat.

Sprawling rustic settlements became organised towns to include councils and law courts. Not forgetting the markets and shops that appeared. The Romans also liked to be clean, and bathing was a huge part of their regular routine. Bath houses were built in a lot of the major towns and cities.

Christianity arrived in Britain during the late 2nd Century but originally only had a small cult following. However, in 260 CE it as given official status as a legitimate religion. It was then that it began to grow as a faith. Christianity became the most popular religion in Britain after 313 CE. Although the Pagan presence survived well into the early 5th Century.

Romans stayed secure in Britain, although the forces were weakened over time, being deployed elsewhere. The Caledonia tribes, called 'Pictii' by the Romans made a serious attempt against the Romans during the 4th century. 367 CE was an important year, The Picts headed southwards, the Scotti crossed over from Ireland. The south and eastern coasts bore Saxons and Franks all aimed towards the Romans. The land was left in chaos filled with slaves, army deserters and Scotti pirates pillaging the countryside. Order was regained in 370 CE by Count Theodosius, he made peace with the tribes and kept everyone busy re-building.

Eventually, of course, Roman Britain fell, there was no specific date, it happened over a period of time. The Roman army were drafted section by section elsewhere leaving very few Roman forces left in Britain. In 407 CE the remainder of the Roman army left Britain to fight elsewhere. 410 CE is the recognised year that Roman Britain ended. In the mid-400s the Roman towns were crumbling and unkept, Germanic type settlements of timber huts with thatched roofs in their place. Plague and famine did the rest.

The Germanic Tribes, the Angles, Saxons and Jutes

During 450–500 CE we saw the arrival of the Germanic tribes, the Angles, Saxons and Jutes. These were the times of the Dark Ages, and we know very little because nothing was written down. What was recorded was documented approximately 100 years later in 540 CE, *The Ruin of Britain* by the monk Gildas.

His writings tell of a British chieftain called Gurthigern or sometimes known as Vortigern. He ruled the south east area of England. To help protect against the raids from the Picts he hired mercenaries in the form of Saxons. With an influx of Germanic warriors, Jutish warlords and their followers, the country was overrun with Angles and Saxons. However, all is perhaps not as gruesome as Gildas would have us believe. Archaeological evidence shows that the numbers of Anglo Saxons that arrived here were not so great and that they co-existed alongside the British, not slaughtering them all.

The British did what we do best, and we rallied together under the rule of Ambrosius Aurelianus. In the late 5th Century he led a campaign against the Saxons. The area of battle being Mons Badonicus, Badon Hill near Bath, Somerset. The campaign was a success. And there followed a long period of peace. It also seems to have inspired a greater understanding and co-operation between the Anglo Saxons and the British. British power continued to spread and by the mid-6th Century the north coast of Cornwall and Yeovil in Somerset had strongholds. Cumbria was ruled by King Urien, you can read about his victory over the Saxons in the Book of Taliesin. What we have been left with is a big ole melting pot of Roman, Germanic and Britons.

Once the Romans left Britain, they left lingering threads of Christianity. Although the kings of southern Britain were Anglo Saxons with Pagan beliefs, Christianity began to filter in led by missionaries bent on converting everyone.

As we enter post-Roman times, the British Isles had a number of separate kingdoms. These were a mixture of Christian and Pagan. Each kingdom battling on a regular basis with the others. Eventually early Anglo Saxon England had seven kingdoms – Kent, Essex, Sussex, Wessex, East Anglia, Mercia and Northumberland. It seems Northumbria, Mercia and Wessex were the most powerful of the kingdoms. Wales held out for a considerable amount of time, but eventually lost to the push from the Anglo Saxons. Scotland continued to be divided into smaller kingdoms. The Votadini tribe became the British kingdom of Gododdin. A lot of northern Scotland remained Pictish.

At the beginning of 500 CE settlers from Germany created a couple of small kingdoms in Britain, finding their home on the east coast. Between the Tweed and the Tyne, they founded Bernicia and Deira which fell between the Tees and the Humber. In 582 CE Aethelfrith added Bernicia to his kingdom and in 604 CE Deira too. He became the founding king of Northumbria. He was a fierce and powerful leader who led and won many battles. Northumbria became a leading force in Britain. During the 630s the Northumbrians successfully integrated the kingdom of Gododdin into their fold and made good headway into the kingdoms of Rheged and Strathclyde. In the 650s they successfully defeated Mercia too. But pretty soon after, the Mercians fought back and won. Plague didn't help with depleting the ranks. In 685 CE they made a move on the Picts above the Firth of Forth. It was to be a terrible decision, leading the Northumbrians to their demise.

Due to the Anglo-Saxon invasions, during the 6th and 7th centuries the Brythonic people of the north and west became separated. Wales began to develop its own community and character. In the 8th century in particular their own identity increased. The Welsh language began to overtake and eventually replace Latin. They also embraced the Christian faith.

In Scotland, from 500 CE, the Scots, Picts, Angles and Britons all fought against each other over the land. North of the Tay the lands were ruled by Picts. In the west the land was held by The Gaels (known later as the Scotti). Strathclyde was held by the British right into the 11th century. It was a long journey for the Scottish to gain back all their lands. The Picts had been Pagan, but somewhere during the 6th and 7th centuries they converted to

Christianity. By 750 CE the Picts held claim to most of Scotland. But by the early 9th century large parts of Northern Scotland were held by Norse. In 843 CE the king of the Scots, Kenneth MacAlpin overran the Picts and became their king. The new kingdom was called Alba (in Gaelic), although the Latin name Scotia was also used. It does seem though, that the Picts and the Scots had a good relationship in trade and with inter tribe marriages too.

The Dark Ages (500–1000) came after the Romans and it was dominated by Christianity and the Church. Our history from this time was written mostly by monks. Abbeys and schools were built and flourished.

The Vikings

And then came the Vikings (790-980). The Danes arrived on our shores in the late 700s, sacking and looting monasteries as they went. By the early 800s they had settled in the Shetlands, Orkneys and along the north and west coasts of Scotland. They also headed to the Irish coast, into Dublin, Westford, Waterford, Cork and Limerick. In 850 CE they moved into north east Kent and then onto the Isle of Sheppey. In 865 CE a large Danish army arrived, referred to as the 'Great Heathen Army'. Within five years they held East Anglia and Northumbria. Reinforcements arrived and they took Mercia. They moved against Wessex, and they nearly had them, but the Wessex forces joined with those of Wiltshire and Somerset and stopped the Vikings from moving further. A treaty was then made creating a border between Wessex and the lands that the Danes held. This became known as the Danelaw.

The English, Scottish and Irish kept battling against the Vikings to gain back their land. By 899 CE Wessex had gained back London, West Mercia and Kent. Just a few short years later York and Northumbria had been reclaimed too. There was a bit of backwards and forwards for a while, but eventually in 954 CE, the last Viking ruler of York, Eric Bloodaxe (such a good name) was killed. You would think that was the end of it, but it wasn't. England had pulled together as a united front. Any Danish that had chosen to settle were filtering into the population with ease. Scotland still had a few invaders to deal with, but they were quickly despatched. Ireland did much the same, coming out on top. And then it happened. In 991 an army of Danish troops arrived in Essex and won the battle. The king decided the best course of action would be to buy off the Danes. He gave them 4500kg/10000lb of silver. This wasn't the last payment, a couple more were made over the next few years, all done to keep the peace. Then in 1002 the king decreed that all Danes should be slaughtered. The massacre happened on 13th November and was named St Brice's Day. Unsurprisingly, this didn't solve the problem, merely aggravated it. Retaliation attacks were sent from Denmark and in 1017, Cnut the Great, a Dane was made King of all England. He ruled for 19 years. Also becoming king of Denmark and Norway too. It seems he did quite a good job as King, building up the trade and churches. After his death and brief stints as king by his sons and then the famous 1066 battle led by Scandinavian troops followed by a couple of other attempts against us, the end of the Viking reign in England was done.

And I am going to finish there. I could go on and on right up to present day, but such a lot happens within that time frame and little of it is Pagan. This seems like a good place to stop. Suffice to say eventually we all came together. I won't say we sorted out our issues and peace ensued, because we know that sadly politics, greed and fight for power still exists. But at least people don't wander around now swinging axes, well at least not often.

Part II
Gods & Goddesses

Gods & Goddesses

The Pantheons

We use the term 'pantheon' taken from the Greek which means 'all the gods'. It helps to describe a collective group of deities from one country or area. When it comes to Britain it gets a bit complicated. We have the Germanic pantheon which includes Norse and Saxon gods and goddesses. Then we have the Celtic pantheon which generally covers Welsh, Scottish and Irish deities. It becomes tricky because we had so many outside influences creating mini pantheons within pantheons such as Romano-Celtic, Saxon-Germanic and Norse-Germanic. And, of course, we are back to the lack of anything written down to support them. Somewhere along the way, the English pantheon got lost and in a lot of cases was assimilated into the Romano-Celtic grouping.

Gods & Goddesses

For some of these deities I have been able to give a fair amount of information. For others all we have is a record of their name, sometimes all that was found was one inscription on a relic or mention in an old manuscript. A lot of what we know came from the Romans who documented the names of a lot of our native deities. Christian monks also recorded a lot of information. Bear in mind that these sources may well have been tainted by their own personal views and beliefs.

If you feel drawn to any particular deity or find one that is in your location, I would encourage you to investigate more. Although research may not bring up much information you can connect on a spiritual level with their energy and see if there is a journey there for you.

When the Romans arrived in Britain, they liked to worship their gods with grand ceremony, and they expected everyone else to do the same. Temples were built to honour their gods such as Juno and Minerva. The deities that were worshipped in Britannia were merged with Roman gods such as Sulis becoming Sulis Minerva and Tuetates becoming Mars Teutates. Eventually the Romans and their trade partners also introduced gods from other countries such as Astarte, Mithras-Sol and, of course, Jesus Christ.

The Anglo Saxons worshipped Germanic and Scandinavian gods and brought that faith with them. Deities that we recognise such as Woden, Thunor and Frige (we now know the first two as Odin and Thor). Bede recorded some Saxon information; other sources include Norse lore such as the Edda verses.

Britain had many travellers from other countries, some were just visiting, others stayed and made their home here. Many of them brought their own deities with them, some of them were then adopted by us.

A lot of our native deities are only mentioned in one town or city, even just connected to one specific river. Perhaps because that was their only place of worship, although they did seem to revere the power and energy of rivers, or maybe any records or stories have been lost in the mists of time. Nature and the landscape seems to have inspired at lot of these gods and goddesses. The Celts in particular did not build temples for their gods, they didn't worship inside buildings. Their connection to deity was made through nature, often in sacred groves of trees or by sacred water. They would probably have also revered gods of the sky, the sun and the moon as well. Fertility would have also played a big part in their spirituality.

Some of the names have variations in spelling, this may have resulted in the Romans recording names and Latinising them. I have included as much information as I could find with my research but I have also added thoughts and insights from my own personal interpretation and experiences with them. Where possible I have included the evidence from archaeological finds.

Generally these are from the Roman period where they took on English deities as their own or, perhaps, they felt it would be of benefit to them to worship the local gods. The fact they did take on the local deities helps us with a record of their names and areas they were worshipped in.

I have included deities from across England, for information on Irish and Welsh deities I can recommend two books: *Gods & Goddesses of Ireland* by Morgan Daimler and *Gods & Goddesses of Wales* by Halo Quin.

Abandinus
God
Location: Godmanchester, Cambridgeshire

Evidence: One single altar stone was found at Godmanchester (Durovigutum). A bronze feather was found with the inscription: 'DEO ABANDION VATIAVCVS D S D' which translates as 'To the god Abandinus, Vatiacus dedicates this out of his own funds.'

Notes: Various suggestions have been made to translate his name, breaking down the Proto-Celtic/Proto-Indo-European elements: 'The god who sings to something/someone', 'The God who binds something/someone to something/someone', 'Andinus of the River' (the Proto-Celtic word 'abon' meaning 'river') or 'Melodious One' (from the Proto-Celtic 'Ad-bandinos').

Aegil
God
Location: Northumbria

Evidence: Mentioned in the Ashbury and Uffington Charter, the Eceles Beorh 'AEgil's Burgh' named after Aegil as the archer brother of the blacksmith god, Weland. A whale bone casket was found believed to be of Northumbrian origin, it is covered in Anglo Saxon art with Christian, Roman, Germanic and Sigurd legend images. One of which is suggested to be the life of Egil/ Aegil. Married to a Valkyrie wife, a Swan Maiden. He is a hero in the Völundarkviða and the Thidreks sagas.

Alaisiagae

Goddesses

Location: Hadrian's Wall, Northumberland

Evidence: Inscriptions on altar stones have been found in the area of Housesteads (Vercovicivm) fort. A buff sandstone altar decorated with a knife, axe, patera (dish) and jug was found with the inscription 'Deo Marti et duabus Alaisiagis et N(umini) Aug(usti) Ger(mani) cives Tuihanti cunei Frisiorum Ver(covicianorum) Se(ve)r(iani) Alexand-riani votum solverunt libent[es] m(erito)' which translates as 'To the god Mars and the two Alaisiagae and to the Divinity of the Emperor the Germans being tribesmen of Twenthe of the cuneus of Frisians of Vercovicium, styled Severus Alexander's, willingly and deservedly fulfilled their vow.'

A buff sandstone pillar decorated with a female figure on one side was found with the inscription 'Deo Marti Thincso et duabus Alaisiagis Bede et Fi-mmilene et N(umini) Aug(usti) Ger-m(ani) cives Tu-ihanti v(otum) s(olverunt) l(ibentes) m(erito)' which translates as 'To the god Mars Thincsus and the two Alaisiagae, Beda and Fimmilena, and to the Divinity of the Emperor the Germans, being tribesmen of Twenthe, willingly and deservedly fulfilled their vow.' A lintel was found matching this which features images of Mars with a sword, shield and spear with a goose beside him. The Alaisiagae sit naked and cross-legged holding palm branches and carrying wreaths.

A buff sandstone altar was found with the inscription 'Deabus Alaisia-gis Bau-dihillie et Friaga-bi et N(umini)

Aug(usti) n(umerus) Hnau-difridi v(otum) s(olvit) l(ibens) m(erito)' which translates as 'To the goddesses the Alaisiagae, Baudihillia and Friagabis, and to the Divinity of the Emperor the unit of Hnaudifridus gladly and deservedly fulfilled its vow.'

Notes: The Alaisagae were thought to be two goddesses of Celtic and/or Germanic origin. Their Celtic names reflecting the Germanic ones in the inscription as Fimmilena and Beda. The collective name Alaisiagae comes from Proto Celtic and means 'sending fears or despatching terrors'. This makes them quite convincingly warrior goddesses of battle. The name Baudihillia translates as 'victory's fullness' and Beda as 'burial'.

Alator
God
Location: Hertfordshire, Durham

Evidence: A buff sandstone altar decorated with a patera (dish) and jug was found at South Shields (Arbeia) with the inscription 'Mar(ti) Ala(tori) G(aius) Vinicius Celsus pro se et [..] v(otum) s(olvit) l(ibens) m(erito)' which translates as 'To Mars Alator, Gaius Vinicius Celsus for himself and ... willingly and deservedly fulfilled his vow.'

A votive gilt silver plaque embossed with a shrine image in the centre, featuring an image of Mars holding a spear and shield, surrounded by a leaf pattern was found at Barkway, Hertfordshire. The inscription reads 'D(eo) Marti Alatori Dum(...) Censorinus Gemelli fil(ius) v(otum) s(olvit) l(ibens) m(erito)' which translates as 'To the god Mars Alator Dum(...) Censorinus, son of Gemellus, willingly and deservedly fulfilled his vow.'

Notes: The Romans equated him to their god Mars. It may mean he was a protector or healer. The name Alator is Celtic and translates as 'huntsman'.

Ancasta
Goddess
Location: Bitterne, Hampshire

Evidence: A stone altar was found in a Roman settlement, Clausentum in Bitterne, Hampshire (near Southampton). The inscription reads 'Deae Anca-stae G-eminu-s Mani (filius) v(otum) s(olvit) l(ibens) m(erito)' which translates as 'To the goddess Ancasta, Geminus, son of Manius, willingly and deservedly fulfilled his vow.' It is as far as we know the only mention of this goddess.

Notes: Her name can be translated to mean 'very swift one' alternatively it could be 'sacred or holy one', although these are just suggestions. It could be that she was a local goddess linked to the river Itchen.

Andescociuoucus
God
Location: Colchester, Essex

Evidence: An inscription was found on a Purbeck marble dedication slab in a ditch on the site of a Roman cemetery near Colchester (Colonia Camulodunum) in Essex. The inscription reads 'Numinib(us) Aug(ustorum) et Mercu(rio) deo Andescoci-uouco Imi-lico Aesuri-lini libertus aram opera maronio d(e) s(uo) d(edit)'. Translated to read 'To the Divinities of the Emperors and to the god Mercury Andescociuoucus, Imilico, freedman of Aesurilinus, from his own resources gave this altar in marble.'

Notes: It seems the God Andescociuoucus was combined with the Roman god Mercury. The word 'Andescoci' means 'the great activator'. Colchester (Camulodunum) was probably the site of the oldest Roman town in Britain. It was certainly an important one. It was the main base for the Trinovantes tribe.

Andred/Andraste
Goddess
Location: Norfolk, Suffolk

Evidence: I give two names here because, originally, she was called Andred, it was the Romans who referred to her as Andraste, but this is the more commonly used name now. The Roman historian Dio Cassius said that Queen Boudicca invoked the goddess Andraste before going into battle with the Iceni tribe. Boudicca's speech taken from Roman History by Cassius Dio:

> *"Let us, therefore, go against them trusting boldly to good fortune. Let us show them that they are hares and foxes trying to rule over dogs and wolves."*

When she had finished speaking, she employed a species of divination, letting a hare escape from the fold of her dress; and since it ran on what they considered the auspicious side, the whole multitude shouted with pleasure, and Boudicca, raising her hand toward heaven, said:

> *"I thank thee, Andraste, and call upon thee as woman speaking to woman; for I rule over no burden-bearing Egyptians as did Nitocris, nor over trafficking Assyrians as did Semiramis (for we have by now gained thus much learning from the Romans!), much less over the Romans themselves as did Messalina once and afterwards Agrippina and now Nero (who, though in name a man, is in fact a woman, as is proved by his singing, lyre-playing and beautification of his person); nay, those over whom I rule are Britons, men that know not how to till the soil or ply a trade,*

but are thoroughly versed in the art of war and hold all things in common, even children and wives, so that the latter possess the same valour as the men.

As the queen, then, of such men and of such women, I supplicate and pray thee for victory, preservation of life, and liberty against men insolent, unjust, insatiable, impious, — if, indeed, we ought to term those people men who bathe in warm water, eat artificial dainties, drink unmixed wine, anoint themselves with myrrh, sleep on soft couches with boys for bedfellows, — boys past their prime at that, — and are slaves to a lyre-player and a poor one too.

Wherefore may this Mistress Domitia-Nero reign no longer over me or over you men; let the wench sing and lord it over Romans, for they surely deserve to be the slaves of such a woman after having submitted to her so long. But for us, Mistress, be thou alone ever our leader."

This seems to be one of the only mentions of this goddess. However, there is an ancient forest in Sussex called 'The Weald', right up to and during Anglo-Saxon times the forest was referred to as 'Andredes Weald' meaning 'the forest of Andred'. Perhaps a site that was sacred to her?

With her connection to the warrior Queen Boudicca, Andred/Andraste has become known as a warrior goddess. Her name could mean 'Victory or Invincible'.

Anextiomarus/Anextlomarus
God
Location: County Durham

Evidence: A bronze bowl was found at South Shields (Arbeia) has an inscription to him.

Notes: His name could be derived from old Irish and mean 'great protector'. The Romans equated him to their god Apollo.

Antenociticus

God

Location: Northumberland

Evidence: A buff sandstone altar was found at Benwell fort (Condercum), Northumberland in a Roman temple. It is decorated with a knife, a jug and three wreaths. The inscription reads 'Deo Antenocitico et Numinib(us) Augustor(um) Ael(ius) Vibius (centurio) leg(ionis) XX V(aleriae) V(ictricis) v(otum) s(olvit) l(ibens) m(erito)'. Translated it reads as 'To the god Antenociticus and to the Divinities of the Emperors Aelius Vibius, centurion of the Twentieth Legion Valeria Victrix, willingly and deservedly fulfilled his vow.'

Three fragments of a buff sandstone altar were found in the same area with the inscription 'Deo An[t]enocitico sacrum coh(ors) I Va[n]gion(um) quib(us) prae est [...]c(ius) Cassi-[anus p]raef(ectus) [v(otum) s(olvit) l(ibens)] m(erito)'. Translated to read 'Sacred to the god Antenociticus: The First Cohort of Vangiones, under the command of ... Cassianus, prefect, willingly and deservedly fulfilled its vow.'

And a third find in the same area was another buff sandstone altar that reads 'Deo Anocitico iudiciis Optimo-rum Maximorum-que Imp(eratorum) N(ostrorum) sub Ulp(io) Marcello co(n)s(ulari) Tine-ius Longus in p[re-] fectura equitu[m] lato clavo exorna-tus et q(uaestor) d(esignatus)'. This translates as 'To the god Anociticus Tineius Longus (set this up) having, while prefect of cavalry, been adorned with the (senatorial) broad stripe and designated quaestor by the decrees of our best and greatest Emperors, under Ulpius Marcellus, consular governor.'

Notes: Although the Benwell fort is no longer visible, there is a temple close by dedicated to the god, Antenociticus which would have originally been inside a settlement. This god is not mentioned in any other location, as far as we know so it is presumed, he was a local deity.

Arecurius
God
Location: Corbridge, Northumberland

Evidence: A buff sandstone base relief of a god (head missing) was found in Corbridge (Coriosopitum). The inscription reads 'Deo Arecurio Apollinaris Cassi (filius) v(otum) s(olvit) l(ibens) m(erito)' which translates as 'To Arecurius, Apollinaris, son of Cassius, willingly and deservedly fulfilled his vow.'

Notes: As the figure bears resemblance to the Roman god Mercury, it was originally thought this was a statue of him with the mason making an error in the inscription. Historians have now come to the conclusion that it isn't Mercury and is an otherwise unknown god, Arecurius. His name translates to mean 'the one who stands before the tribe'.

Arnemetia
Goddess
Location: Buxton, Derbyshire

Evidence: A gritstone altar with focus and bolsters was found in the strong room of the Navio Roman fort at Brough-on-Noe, Derbyshire. The inscription reads 'Deae Arnomecte Ael(ius) Motio v(otum) s(olvit) l(aetus) l(ibens) m(erito)'. It translates as 'To the goddess Arnomecta Aelius Motio gladly, willingly, and deservedly fulfilled his vow.' The inscription is circled by an engraved wreath with ribbons.

Notes: Although to me, it looks like the 'wreath' could be a cauldron or even a chalice shape, but that's purely my interpretation. The town of Buxton Spa in Derbyshire was called Aquae Arnemetiae during Roman times. Her name translates as 'she who dwells over the sacred grove'. Sacred grove being the term 'nemeton'. It seems she could have been the goddess who ruled over the sacred waters of Buxton.

Barrecis/Barrex
God
Location: Carlisle, Cumbria

Evidence: Just one reference (that we know of) to this god, found on a buff sandstone altar at Carlisle (Luguvalium). The inscription reads 'M(arti) Bar-regi Ia-nuari-us Ri[ ]-regipau v(otum) s(olvit) l(ibens) m(erito)'. This translates as 'To Mars Barrex Januarius Ri[.]regipau... willingly and deservedly fulfilled his vow.'

Notes: The inscription does link him to the Roman god, Mars. The name Barrecis means 'supreme one'. Carlisle (Luguvalium) which was the capital for the Carvetii tribe.

Belatucadros
God
Location: Cumbria, Northumberland, North Yorkshire

Evidence: Several items have been found at Brougham (Brocavum) fort in Cumbria that make reference to Belatucadros.

A stone altar or statue base bears the inscription 'd[eo] sancto Belatu-catro votum' which means 'To the holy god Belatucatrus, a vow (fulfilled).'

A buff sandstone altar was found at Carvoran (Magnis) fort, Northumberland bearing the inscription 'Deo Balit-icau-ro v-otu(m)' which translates as 'To the god Baliticaurus a vow.'

A red sandstone altar was found in Carlisle (Luguvalium)

showing the inscription 'Deo Marti Belatucadro' which translates as 'To the god Mars Belatucadrus.'

A red sandstone altar was found at Netherby (Castra Exploratorum), North Yorkshire that states 'Deo Marti Belatucadro {RO} [A]ur(elius(?)) [Ni(?)]ca[n(?)-] or v(otum) s(olvit) [l(aetus) l(ibens)] m(erito)' which translates as 'To Mars Belatucadrus Aurelius Nicanor gladly, willingly, and deservedly fulfilled his vow.'

A red sandstone altar found at Kirkby Thore (Bravoniacum) bears the inscription 'Deo Belatucad-ro lib(ens) votu-m fecit [.]iolus which translates as 'To the god Belatucadrus [...]iolus willingly fulfilled his vow'.

At the Old Penrith (Voreda) site a red sandstone altar was found that states 'Deo sa-ncto Belat-ucai-ro po(suit)' which translates as 'To the holy god Belatucairus (...) erected (this altar)'.

Notes: There are more of these examples, all along the same lines, he was clearly highly thought of. His name translates as 'bright or fair shining one'. A few of the inscriptions mention him in tandem with the Roman god Mars. Some sources suggest he should be compared to the god Belenus. However, as there are more items that name just him, I suspect he was a strong deity in his own right. Baliticauro and Belatucauro seem to be variants of Belatucadro.

Belenus

God

Location: Durham, Lancashire

Evidence: Mention of Belenus or under the spelling Bellinus is made on a buff sandstone building stone found at Piercebridge (Moribum) in Durham. The inscription simply states 'Bellinus' and you don't need a translation for that!

A broken stone altar found at Overborough, Lancashire bears

the text '[Nu]minib(us) [Au]g(usti) n(ostri) et Ge-[ni]o COLGF [A]poll[i]nis [B]ellinus v(otum) s(olvit) l(ibens) m(erito)' which translates as 'To the Divinities of our Emperor and the Genius of the guild of Apollo Bellinus willingly and deservedly fulfilled his vow.'

Notes: This shows us that the Romans equated Belenus with their god, Apollo. Mention of him is made in various ancient texts from across Europe. At the Roman Baths in Bath, Somerset you will see what was originally thought to be a stone gorgon's head found above the temple of the goddess Sulis. It is now thought to be a depiction of the god Belenus. He is believed to have been widely worshipped throughout Britain and Europe. His name translates as 'bright or shining one'.

Belisama
Goddess
Location: Lancashire

Evidence: Belisama had quite a cult following in France that may well have travelled over into Britain. Ptolemy noted the 'Belisama estuary' which referred to what we know as the River Ribble in Lancashire. Perhaps the site of a Belisama cult following in England.

Notes: Her name possibly means 'the brightest one' or 'the powerful one'. It seems the Romans linked her with their goddess Minerva, giving her the name Minervae Belissimae. Stories relate her to the element of fire and see her as a battle goddess.

Black Annis
Goddess?
Location: Leicestershire

Evidence: I have included Black Annis, although probably not a goddess, more of a folk story. I do think she may have been inspired by the goddess The Cailleach, who features prominently in Scotland and Ireland. Black Annis lived in a cave in the side of the Dane Hills which is just outside of the city of Leicester. Although now built up, it used to be a series of low sandstone hills, which held a small cave known by the locals as Black Annis' Bower. She was said to be an old hag with long claws that captured children and sucked their blood, hanging their skins up to dry outside of her cave. She sounds lovely...

Braciaca
God
Location: Bakewell, Derbyshire

Evidence: A gritstone altar was found in Bakewell, Derbyshire bearing the inscription 'Deo
Marti Braciacae Q(uintus) Sittius Caecilian(us) praef(ectus) coh(ortis) I Aquitano(rum) v(otum) s(olvit)' which translates as 'To the god Mars Braciaca, Quintus Sittius Caecilianus, prefect of the First Cohort of Aquitanians, fulfilled his vow.'

Notes: The suggestion is his name translates as 'God of malt', however, Braciacus was also a place name in Gaul. The inscription mentions Mars, so we assume the Romans equated him with their god Mars.

Bregans
God
Location: West Yorkshire

Evidence: A sandstone altar was found at Slack in West Yorkshire, just east of the Roman Cambodunum (Slack) fort. The inscription reads 'Deo Breganti et N(umini) Aug(usti) T(itus)

Aur(elius) Quintus d(ono) d(edit) p(ecunia) et s(umptu) s(uo)'
which translates as 'To the god Bregans and the Divinity of the
Emperor, Titus Aurelius Quintus gave this as a gift by his own
funds and expense.'

Notes: The suggestion is that Bregans is the masculine form of
Brigantia. The name translates the same as 'high one'. He could
be a consort to Brigantia and seen as the god of the Brigantes
tribe. Ptolemy noted this site as one of the bases for the Brigantes
tribe.

Brigantia
Goddess
Location: Yorkshire, Northumberland, Tyne and Wear

Evidence: There are several finds of note that mention Brigantia.

A sandstone altar with a serpent design was found at the
Roman site Adel, Leeds in West Yorkshire. The inscription reads
'Deae Brigan(tiae) d(onum) Cinge-tissa p(osuit)' which translates
as 'To the goddess Brigantia, Cingetissa set up this offering.'

Another stone altar was discovered at Castleford
(Lagentium), West Yorkshire bearing the inscription 'Deae Vic-
toriae Brigant(iae) a(ram) d(edicavit) Aur(elius) S-enopianus'
which translates as 'To the goddess Victoria Brigantia Aurelius
Senopianus dedicated this altar.'

A buff sandstone altar decorated with a crowned Genius
with a right hand held above an altar and the left hand holding
a cornucopia together with a winged cupid holding a sickle and
a bunch of grapes. On either side were medallions. This was
discovered at Corbridge (Coria/Corstopitum), Northumberland
the site of a Roman fort, but previously Iron Age round houses.
The inscription reads 'Iovi aeterno Dolicheno et Caelesti
Brigantiae et Saluti G(aius) Iulius Ap-olinaris (centurio)
leg(ionis) VI iuss(u) dei' which translates as 'To eternal Jupiter

of Doliche and to Caelestis Brigantia and to Salus Gaius Julius Apolinaris, centurion of the Sixth Legion, at the command of the god (set this up).'

In Greetland, West Yorkshire an altar stone was discovered, on the site of a possible rural shrine. The inscription reads 'D(eae) Vict(oriae) Brig(antiae) et Num(inibus) Aug(ustorum) T(itus) Aur(elius) Aurelian-us d(edit) d(edicavit) pro se et suis s(e) mag(istro) s(acrorum) Antonin[o] III et Geta [II] co(n)s(ulibu) s' which translates as 'To the goddess Victoria Brigantia and to the Divinities of the two Emperors, Titus Aurelius Aurelianus gave and dedicated (this altar) for himself and his family, while he himself was master of sacred rites, in the third consulship of Antoninus and the [second] of Geta.'.

A sandstone altar was found at Hadrian's Wall with the inscription 'Deae Nymphae Brig(antiae) quod [vo]verat pro sal[ute et incolumitate] dom(ini) nostr(i) Invic(ti) imp(eratoris) M(arci) Aurel(i) Severi Antonini Pii Felic[i]s Aug(usti) totiusque do-mus divinae eius M(arcus) Cocceius Nigrinus [pr]oc(urator) Aug(usti) n(ostri) devo-[tissim]us num[ini] [maies]tatique eius v(otum) [s(olvit)] l(aetus) l(ibens) m(erito)' which translates as 'This offering to the goddess-nymph Brigantia, which he had vowed for the welfare and safety of our Lord the Invincible Emperor Marcus Aurelius Severus Antoninus Pius Felix Augustus and of his whole Divine House, Marcus Cocceius Nigrinus, procurator of our Emperor and most devoted to his divinity and majesty, gladly, willingly, and deservedly fulfilled.'

A buff sandstone altar was discovered at South Shields (Arbeia) Roman Fort. It is decorated with a bird, patera and a jug. The inscription reads 'Deae Bri-gantiae sacrum Congenn(i) c-cus v(otum) s(olvit) l(ibens) m(erito)' which translates as 'Sacred to the goddess Brigantia: Congennicus willingly and deservedly fulfilled his vow.'

Notes: Her name translates as 'high one'. Several rivers seem to have been named after her. The Romans equated her to two of their goddesses, Victoria and Minerva (that Minerva sure gets around).

Brigantia is seen as the goddess of the Brigantes tribe.

Britannia
Goddess
Location: Yorkshire

Evidence: A gritstone statue base was found in York (Eburacum/ Colonia Eboracensis) fort. The top of which had traces of lead that presumably held a statue in place on top. The inscription reads 'Britanniae Sanctae p(osuit) Nikomedes Aug(ustorum) N(ostrorum) libertus' which translates as 'To Holy Britannia Nikomedes, freedman of our Emperors, set (this) up.'

Notes: This name might seem familiar to you, as it was the name the Romans gave to Britain. Britannia became the symbol and representation of the British Empire. She is seen as protector and guardian of Britain but also embodies the spirit of the British people often depicted as a warrior wearing a helmet and carrying a trident and shield.

You will find Britannia featured on old Roman coins and then she appears on British coinage in 1672. Her image has been depicted on British coins ever since. Ptolemy lists York as one of the bases for the Brigantes tribe.

Callirius
God
Location: Colchester, Essex

Evidence: A bronze plate was found at Colchester (Colonia Camulodunum). The inscription reads 'Deo Silvano Callirio d(onum) Cintusmus aerarius v(otum) s(olvit) l(ibens) m(erito)' which translates as 'To the god Silvanus Callirius, Cintusmus, the coppersmith, willingly and deservedly fulfilled as a gift his vow.'

Notes: Although a lot of the names of those that make the inscriptions are usually Roman, the name Cintusmus on the bronze plate is a Celtic name. Silvanus is a Roman god of nature, woodlands and animals. The suggestion has been made that the name Callirius derives from the Celtic 'kalli' from the root 'kel' meaning that his name is that of the woods. This makes sense as that would make him God of the woods and therefore very apt to be aligned with the Roman god Silvanus. Colchester (Colonia Camulodunum) was a base for the Trinovantes tribe and then the Catuvellauni.

Camulos
God
Location: Colchester, Essex

Evidence: The Roman name for the town of Colchester in Essex is Camulodunum, this is the Roman version of the original name Camulodunon. The thought is that it means 'the fort of Camulos'. We don't have much information to go on, his possible image does appear on a few coins from Gaul pressed during the imperial Roman period. These coins show a man with stag horns and a boar by his side. One altar piece has been found up in Scotland that mentions the god 'To the god Mars Camulus the soldiers of the First Cohort of Hamians'.

Notes: The Romans equated Camulos to their god Mars. Perhaps he was more of a protector or hunter god than a war one like Mars? Camulos was believed to have been worshipped by the Belgae and Remi tribes.

Cocidius

God

Location: Cumbria, Northumberland, various sites along Hadrian's Wall, Lancashire, Yorkshire, Co. Durham

Evidence: Numerous dedications and inscriptions have been found naming Cocidius. Five altars found at Bewcastle (Fanum Cocidi) fort were dedicated to Cocidius and one other to Mars Cocidius. A silver embossed plaque from Bewcastle showing Cocidius standing in a shrine holding a spear and a shield. The inscription reads 'Deo Cocidio', meaning 'To the god Cocidius'.

Another silver embossed plaque from Bewcastle shows Cocidisu standing holding a spear. The inscription reads 'Deo D(e)o Coc(i)dio Av(e)ntinus f(ecit)' translated as 'To the god: to the god Cocidius Aventinus set this up.'

Most of the altars found at Bewcastle bear inscriptions to 'the holy god Cocidius' and then the name of the legionary centurion. Other stone altars have been found at various sites along Hadrian's Wall, Housesteads, Castlesteads, Birdoswald, Vindolanda, Risingham and at other sites in Wallsend, Ebchester and Netherby. Most of them with similar inscriptions such as this one from Castlesteads which reads 'Deo Cocidio milites leg(ionis) VI Vic(tricis) P(iae) F(idelis)' and translates as 'To the god Cocidius the soldiers of the Sixth Legion Victrix Pia Fidelis (set this up).'

Notes: The suggestion being the name of the fort 'Fanum Cocidi' means 'The Shrine of Cocidius'. Cocidius is thought to be a god of war and was favoured by soldiers. The Romans equated him to their god Mars. It is clear he was very popular.

Condatis

God

Location: Durham

Evidence: A buff sandstone altar was found at Chester-le-Street (Concangium/Concangis) just north of the fort. The inscription reads 'Deo Marti Condati V(alerius) [P]rob[i]anus [pr]o se et suis v(otum) s(olvit) l(ibens) m(erito)' which translates as 'To the god Mars Condates, Valerius Probianus for himself and his household willingly and deservedly fulfilled his vow.'

A gritstone altar was found at Bowes (Lavatrae/Lavatris), Durham just east of the fort. The inscription reads 'Mart[i] [...] [M]arti Condati Arponat-us v(otum) s(olvit) l(ibens) m(erito)' and translates as 'To Mars [... . - To Mars Condates Arponatus willingly and deservedly fulfilled his vow.'

A buff sandstone altar was found at Piercebridge, Durham. The inscription reads 'D(eo) M(arti) Condati Attonius Quintianus men(sor) eνϙc(atus) imp(eratum) ex ius(su) sol(vit) l(ibens) a(nimo)and translates as 'To the god Mars Condates, Attonius Quintianus, surveyor, evocatus, gladly fulfilled the command by order.' An evocatus was a soldier of the praetorian guard retained after 16 years' service for special service which might include promotion to centurion and above.

Notes: The word 'condates' means 'watersmeet' in Celtic, perhaps he was seen as a healing god of the waterways. Although I have also seen suggestion that the name translates as 'the joiner together'. The Romans equated him to their god Mars.

Contrebis

God
Location: Lancashire

Evidence: A gritstone altar was found at Lancaster, decorated with a knife on the right side and an axe on the left. The inscription reads 'Deo Ialono Contre(bi) sanctiss[i-] mo Iuliu[s] Ianuarius em(eritus) ex dec(urione) v(otum) [s(olvit)]' which translates as 'To the most holy god Ialonus Contrebis Julius

Januarius, emeritus, former decurion, [fulfilled] his vow.' In this instance he is mentioned together with another relatively unknown god, Ialonus.

A stone altar decorated with a bird, possibly an owl on the right and a hatchet and knife on the left was found at Overborough fort, Lancashire. The inscription reads 'Deo san(cto) Contr-ebi Vat-ta posu(it)' which translates as 'To the holy god Contrebis Vatta set this up.'

Notes: His name Contrebis seems to derive from 'contre' meaning 'of those who dwell together'.

Corotiacus
God
Location: Suffolk

Evidence: One copper alloy statuette base mentions the name Corotiacus, found at Martlesham in Suffolk. It is in the shape of a shield and inscribed around the rim. The only part of the statuette remaining is the stump of a right foot which looks like a horse's hoof and a now headless foeman, laying down. The inscription reads 'Deo Marti Corotiaco Simplicia pro se v(otum) p(osuit) l(ibens) m(erito)' translating as 'To Mars Corotiacus Simplicia for herself willingly and deservedly set up this offering.' On the base it reads 'Glaucus fecit' which is 'Glaucus made it'.

Notes: Corotiacus seems to be yet another god that the Romans equated to their god Mars. The suggestion has been made that Corotiacus was a god of battle.

Coventina
Goddess
Location: Northumberland

Evidence: A number of dedications and altars made to Coventina have been found at Carrawburgh (Brocolitia) in Northumberland. Ten altar and votive stones have been found here dedicated to Coventina, seen as a water nymph.

A buff sandstone dedication featuring an image of a water goddess bears the inscription 'Deae Covventinae T(itus) D(...) Cosconia-nus pr(aefectus) coh(ortis) I Bat(avorum) l(ibens) m(erito)' which translates as 'To the goddess Covventina Titus D(...) Cosconianus, prefect of the First Cohort of Batavians, willingly and deservedly (fulfilled his vow).' Most of the dedications are along the same lines.

A buff sandstone altar reads 'Die Cove-ntine A-urelius Crotus German(us)' translating as 'To the goddess Coventina Aurelius Crotus, a German, (fulfilled his vow).'

Another buff sandstone altar reads 'Deae Nim-fae Coven-tine Mad-uhus Germ(anus) pos(uit) pro se et su(is) v(otum) s(olvens) l(ibens) m(erito)' translating as 'To the goddess-nymph Coventina Maduhus, a German, set this up for himself and his family, willingly and deservedly fulfilling his vow.' A clay incense burner was also found, the inscriptions were made on four sides forming a panel, flanked by columns with a triangle gable above. The inside of the bowl is blacked from use. The inscription reads 'Cove-tina(e) A(u)-gusta(e) votu(m) man-ibus suis Satu-rni-nus fecit Gabi-nius' which translates as 'For Covetina Augusta Saturninus Gabinius made this votive offering with his own hands.'

Notes: Brocolitia consisted of a fort, baths and a Roman settlement including several temples. A natural spring consecrated to Coventina runs beside the fort and an iron-age well dedicated to her which consisted of a large square temple building. In the late 1800's her well was excavated and around 14,000 ancient coins and carved stones were found, all presumably given as offerings to her. We can assume she was a water goddess and very highly thought of by the local community, then taken on board by the Romans. Use of the terms 'Sancta' which means 'holy' and 'Augusta' which means 'revered' shows she was held in high esteem.

Cuda
Goddess
Location: Cirencester, Gloucestershire

Evidence: An oolite relief was found in Daglingworth, Cirencester. Although slightly damaged and weathered it shows a seated goddess on the right with a round object in her lap. In front of her stand three cloaked hooded figures. The first holds what seems to be an offering. There doesn't seem to be any mention of a goddess by this name in any other place. The suggestion is the seated figure is a mother goddess and the three figures are genii cucullati, with the goddess being one of abundance and prosperity.

Notes: Genii cucullate appear in much of Romano-Celtic situations. The term translates as 'hooded or cloaked spirits' they are usually seen in sets of three. The area of Cirencester was a stronghold of the Dobunni tribe.

Eostra/Eostre
Goddess
Location: Northumbria

Evidence: Whilst there doesn't seem to be any physical evidence of this goddess, she is mentioned in the writings of Bede who told of Anglo-Saxons in Northumbria holding festivals to the goddess. He suggests that the first month of spring (April), Eostre-month was named after her. In 1835 Jacob Grimm (of the Brothers Grimm) wrote about Eostre being 'the divinity of the radiant dawn, of upspringing light'. He suggested that she was a local goddess derived from a more widespread deity that he referred to as Ostara.

Epona
Goddess
Location: Northumberland, North Yorkshire

Evidence: A buff sandstone altar was found at Carvoran (Magnis) in Northumberland, thought to be the market centre for the Dobunni tribe. The inscription reads 'Deae Epon-ae P(...) So(...)' which translates as 'To the goddess Epona P(...) So(...) (set this up).'

A partial white sandstone altar was found at Netherby (Castra Exploratorum) with the inscription 'D D(eo(?)) s(ancto(?)) E(...) IVNLIIAR Monime PRID VNICI [.] ERESIS PLERIVM [.] A-RIVS posuit' which translates as 'To the holy deity ... Monime ... set this up.' Unfortunately the name of the deity isn't clear, although it certainly begins with an E, the general belief is that it could be Epona.

A copper alloy figure of Epona seated with a small pony on either side of her was found in Wiltshire. Although looking at the statue, to me they look more like dogs, but I am not a historian!

A small stone sculpture was found in Colchester showing Epona riding a horse.

Notes: She is mentioned in several ancient texts and many other inscriptions have been found for her across Gaul, Germany, the Danubian provinces and in Rome. She was originally from Gaul but is now generally classed in the Celtic pantheon. Her name in Celtic translates as 'Epos' meaning 'horse' and 'ona' means 'on'. In most depictions of her she is seen on a horse or with a horse.

Erce
Goddess
Location: Unknown

Evidence: The goddess Erce is mentioned once, in a single document. The Æcerbot manuscript which is believed to date to the 7th Century. It contains both Heathen and Christian information.

The text in reference to Erce is in the form of an Anglo-Saxon prayer or ritual which includes some rare Old English words that were usually only found in ritual or magical content. It gives instructions on how to make offerings to the land and reads almost like a spell with ritual instructions. It includes giving praise to Christ and Saint Mary but the part we are interested in, translated, reads as follows:

> *Erce! Erce! Erce! Mother of Earth!*
> *May the All-Ruler grant you, the eternal Lord,*
> *Fields growing and flourishing,*
> *Propagating and strengthening,*
> *Tall stems, bright crops,*
> *And broad barley crops,*
> *And white wheat crops,*
> *And all the Earth's crops.*

Notes: If Erce was indeed a goddess then it seems she would have been called upon to bless the earth and bring fertility to the land.

Helith
God
Location: South West England

Evidence: No physical evidence has been found referring to a god named Helith, but there are several mentions of him in medieval and later documents as an Anglo-Saxon deity. Gotselin, a Benedictine monk mentions 'Helio and his followers'. A 13th century English monk, Walter of Coventry writes about the god Gelith who was 'once worshipped' in the county of Dorset. In the 1500's poet John Leland wrote 'the god Helith was worshipped in the village of Cernel in the time of Augustine.'

Notes: There are several variations on what his name translates to. Helia(e) from Middle English 'heil' translates as health, welfare and good fortune. The Old English 'helep' meaning warrior or hero. The Old Saxon 'helio' derives from Proto-Germanic meaning 'hero, warrior or free man'. Helith is the modern version of the Middle English word Helio.

Herne
God
Location: Windsor, Berkshire

Evidence: Herne has an unusual story that puts him in the realm of the gods. There is no physical evidence that he was worshipped as such. His written record was first seen in Shakespeare's work, *The Merry Wives of Windsor*. However, Shakespeare based the character on a myth about a ghost hunter who can be found in the forest at Windsor Great Park. The story dates back to the reign of King Richard II (late 1300's). The King and Herne were out hunting and broke away from the main hunting party. They spotted a white stag and Herne managed to shoot it with an arrow, but only to wound it. They chased after the stag, eventually cornering it, at which point the stag charged at the King. Herne leapt in front of him to save the King. Herne managed to kill the stag with his knife but lost his own life in the process. The King was beside himself with grief and called upon the hunting party for help. A wizard stepped up and offered to bring Herne back from the dead, but it would mean Herne would lose all his hunting skills. The wizard administered plants and potions to the dead Herne and placed the horns from the dead stag onto Herne's head. Herne came back to life, but without any of his hunting skills. He did not deal well with his loss and went mad, eventually running into the forest and hanged himself from a large oak tree. This is just one version of the tale, there are many variations. His ghost has been seen in the form of a stag or as Herne himself. Herne is said to ride in the night along with the Wild Hunt, through the forest particularly on stormy nights. The Wild Hunt prey on those who are wicked, collecting their souls. Unfortunately, the innocent sometimes get caught up with them too. The Wild Hunt has roots in Norse and Germanic beliefs.

Hreda
Goddess
Location: Unknown

Evidence: There is no physical evidence for this goddess. The information we have comes from our friend the monk, Bede. He mentions Rheda (a latinised version of Hreda) as an Anglo-Saxon deity connecting her name to the month of March, or 'Hredmonath'.

Notes: Her name may translate as 'glory' or 'victorious'.

Ialonus
God
Location: Lancashire

Evidence: A gritstone altar with the base broken off, decorated with a knife and an axe was found at Lancaster. The inscription reads 'Deo Ialono Contre(bi) sanctiss[i-] mo Iuliu[s] Ianuarius em(eritus) ex dec(urione) v(otum) [s(olvit)]'. The translation is 'To the most holy god Ialonus Contrebis Julius Januarius, emeritus, former decurion, [fulfilled] his vow.' The word 'contre' mentioned in the inscription is a district name meaning 'of those who dwell together'.

Notes: His name translates to 'god of the meadowland'.

Latis
Goddess
Location: Hadrian's Wall, Cumbria

Evidence: A buff sandstone altar decorated with a jug and patera (libation dish) was found at Birdoswald (Banna) fort. The inscription reads 'Die Lat[i]' which means 'To the goddess Latis'.

A red sandstone altar was found at Burgh-by-Sands (Aballava) fort. The inscription reads 'Deae Lati Lucius Ursei (filius)' which translates as 'To the goddess Latis, Lucius son of Urseius (set this up).'

Notes: Her name may derive from the Proto Celtic word 'lati' meaning 'liquor or liquid'. Basically a beer goddess then.

Loucetius/Leucetius
God
Location: Bath, Somerset

Evidence: An oolite altar with the capital broken off was found at Bath (Aquae Sulis). The inscription reads 'Peregrinus Secundi fil(ius) civis Trever Loucetio Marti et Nemetona v(otum) s(olvit) l(ibens) m(erito)' which translates as 'Peregrinus, son of Secundus, a Treveran, to Loucetius Mars and Nemetona willingly and deservedly fulfilled his vow.'

Notes: His name may derive from the Proto Celtic 'louk(k)et' meaning 'light'. Evidence from north east Gaul shows Mars Loucetius and Nemetona were sometimes worshipped together.

Maponus
God

Location: Northumberland, Cumbria, Lancashire

Evidence: A buff sandstone altar was found at Corbridge (Coria/ Corstopitum) depicting Apollo with a lyre and laurel and Dian with a bow and quiver. The inscription reads [Ap]ollini Mapon[o] [Calpu]rnius [...] trib(unus) dedicavit' which translates as 'To Apollo Maponus, Calpurnius ..., tribune, dedicated this.'

A buff sandstone altar found at Corbridge which had been cut to form a rounded arch, obscuring part of the wording. The inscription reads [Deo] [M]apo[no] Apo[llini] P(ublius) Ae[.. ...]-lus (centurio) [leg(ionis) VI] [V]ic(tricis) v(otum) [s(olvit) l(ibens) m(erito)]'. Translated to read 'To the god Maponus Apollo, Publius Aelius ..., centurion of the Sixth Legion Victrix, willingly and deservedly fulfilled his vow.'

Also at Corbridge, a buff altar sandstone was found reading 'Apollini Mapono Q(uintus) Terentius Q(uinti) f(ilius) Ouf(entina) (tribu) Firmus Saen(a) praef(ectus) castr(orum) leg(ionis) VI V(ictricis) P(iae) F(idelis) d(edit) d(edicavit)' which translates as 'To Apollo Maponus, Quintus Terentius Firmus, son of Quintus, of the Oufentine voting-tribe, from Saena, prefect of the camp of the Sixth Legion Victrix Pia Fidelis, gave and dedicated this.'

A red sandstone altar was found at Hadrian's Wall, near Brampton which reads 'Deo Mapono et n(umini) Aug(usti) Durio et Ramio et Trupo et Lurio Germa-ni v(otum) s(olverunt) l(ibentes) m(erito)' which translates as 'To the god Maponus and to the Divinity of the Emperor the Germans Durio and Ramio and Trupo and Lurio willingly and deservedly fulfilled their vow.'

A stone pedestal shaft was found at Ribchester (Bremetennacum). The decorations show Apollo with a quiver and lyre. Two female figures face each other one partly naked and the other fully draped and veiled. The female figures are believed to represent Regio Bremetennacensis (centered at Ribchester) and Britannia Inferior (lower Britain). The inscription reads 'Deo san(cto) [A]pollini Mapon(o) [pr]o salute D(omini) N(ostri) [et] n(umeri) eq(uitum) Sar-[m(atarum)] Bremetenn(acensium) [G]ordiani [A]el(ius) Antoni-nus (centurio) leg(ionis) VI Vic(tricis) domo Melitenis praep(ositus) et pr(aefectus) v(otum) s(olvit) l(ibens) m(erito) [de]dic(atum) pr(idie) Kal(endas) Sep(tembres) [im]p(eratore) d(omino) n(ostro) Gord[i-] [ano A]ug(usto) II e[t] Pon-[peia]no co(n) s(ulibus)' which translates as 'To the holy god Apollo Maponus for the welfare of our Lord (the Emperor) and of Gordian's Own Unit of Sarmatian cavalry of Bremetennacum Aelius Antoninus, centurion of the Sixth Legion Victrix, from Melitene, acting-commander and prefect, fulfilled his vow willingly, deservedly. Dedicated 31 August in the consulship of the Emperor Our Lord Gordian for the second time and of Ponpeianus.'

Notes: His name derives from the Gaulish and Brittonic 'mapos' which means 'boy'. He is seen as a god of 'divine youth'. The Romans obviously equated him to their god Apollo. He may well have been a god of the Parisii tribe.

Matres/Mothers
Goddesses
Location: Across Britain

Evidence: There are many inscriptions made to the Matres or Mothers found across Britain. Usually made in dedications to a particular country, area or specific role such as 'household mothers'. Similar evidence has been found across Europe. I won't share all the inscriptions here because there are a lot, but here is a selection.

A buff sandstone altar found at Housesteads (Vercovicium), Northumberland with the inscription '[Ma]tribus coh(ors) I Tungr-[or]u[m]' which translates as 'To the Mother Goddesses the First Cohort of Tungrians ... .'

A buff sandstone altar was found at Hadrian's Wall with the inscription 'Ma[tribus] Ger[manis] M(arcus) Senec[i-] [a]nius V[...' which translates as 'To the German Mother Goddesses Marcus Senecianius V ...'.

A stone altar found at Skinburness, Cumbria bears the inscription 'Matribu[s] Par(cis(?)) VITI VACI [..]' which translates as 'To the Mothers the Fates ...'.

A piece of a buff sandstone altar was found at Binchester (Vinovia), Durham with the inscription 'Mat[ribus] trib(us) [...] inst(ante) [..] IRI [..]' which translates as 'To the Three Mothers ... under the direction of ... .'.

A weathered buff sandstone altar was found at Carrawburgh (Brocolitia), Northumberland with the inscription 'Matribus Albinius Quart(us) mil(es) d(edicavit)' which translates as 'To the Mother Goddesses Albinius Quartus, a soldier, dedicated this.'

A red sandstone altar was found at Burgh by Sands, Cumbria with the inscription 'Matri(bus) Dom(esticis) vex(illatio) [l] eg(ionis) VI [V(ictricis)] P(iae) F(idelis)' which translates as 'To the Mother Goddesses of the household a detachment of the Sixth Legion Victrix Pia Fidelis (set this up).'

A buff sandstone dedication showing an image of three Mother Goddesses each on a throne was found at Newcastle upon Tyne (Pons Aelius) with the inscription 'Dea(bus) Matribus Tramarinis Patri(i)s Aurelius Iuvenalis s(acrum)' which translates as 'To the Mother Goddesses of his native land from overseas Aurelius Juvenalis made this offering.'

A stone altar was found at York (Eboracum/Colonia Eboracensis) with the inscription 'Mat(ribus) Af(ris) Ita(lis) Ga(llis) M(arcus) Minu(cius) Aude(n)s mil(es) leg(ionis) VI

Vic(tricis) guber(nator) leg(ionis) VI v(otum) s(olvit) l(aetus) l(ibens) m(erito)' which translates as 'To the African, Italian, and Gallic Mother Goddesses Marcus Minucius Audens, soldier of the Sixth Legion Victrix and a pilot of the Sixth Legion, willingly, gladly, and deservedly fulfilled his vow.'

A red sandstone altar was found at Castlesteads (Camboglanna) with the inscription '[Deabu]s [Mat]ribu[s] omnium gentium templum olim vetus-tate conlab-sum G(aius) Iul(ius) Cu-pitianus (centurio) p(rae)p(ositus) restituit' which translates as 'To the Mother Goddesses of all nations Gaius Julius Cupitianus, centurion in command, restored their temple fallen in through age.'

A purbeck marble slab was found at Chichester (Noviomagus Reg(i)norum) with the inscription '[Matri]bu[s] Domest(icis) [5-6]us ark(arius) [d(e) s(ua)] p(ecunia)' which translates as 'To the Mother Goddesses of Home. [...]us, Treasurer, (erected this) at his own expense.'

A sandstone altar was found at Winchester (Venta Belgarum) with the inscription 'Matrib(us) Italis Ger-manis Gal(lis) Brit(annis) [A]ntonius [Lu]cretianus [b(ene)]f(iciarius) co(n)s(ularis) rest(ituit)' which translates as 'To the Italian, German, Gallic, and British Mother Goddesses Antonius Lucretianus, beneficiarius consularis, restored (this).' Beneficiarius Consularis was an officer on the governor's staff.

Notes: The finds that interest me most and in particular for this book about English deities are what have been called 'The Three Mothers of Cirencester' based on the findings from archaeological digs in and around Ashcroft in Cirencester, Gloucestershire in an area referred to as The Cotswolds.

The number of items discovered at this site and others locally indicates there was a large temple or shrine dedicated to the mothers or Matres. It has been suggested that a cult in and around Roman Corinium (Cirencester) worshipped the

Matres. The images seem to depict three women of similar age, perhaps sisters.

Matunus
God
Location: Northumberland

Evidence: A buff sandstone dedication slab was found at High Rochester (Bremenium). The town was a centre for the Otalini (Votadini) tribe. The inscription reads 'Deo Matuno pro salute M(arci) [A]ur[eli ...] [...] bono generis humani impe-rante G(aius) [Iulius Marcus] leg(atus) Aug(usti) pr(o) pr(aetore) posuit ac dedicavit c(uram) a(gente) Caecil(io) Optato trib(uno)' which translates as 'To the god Matunus for the welfare of Marcus Aurelius ..., reigning for the good of the human race, Gaius Julius Marcus, emperor's propraetorian legate, set up and dedicated this, under the charge of Caecilius Optatus, tribune.'

Notes: His name is thought to be derived from the Proto-Celtic 'matu' meaning 'bear'. With the name association it is thought he may have been a bear god.

Medigenus
God
Location: Norfolk

Evidence: Several silver spoons were found in the Thetford Hoard; each one has an inscription to a god named Faunus Medigenus. A silver spoon decorated with a duck handle, holding a cake in its beak bears the inscription 'DEIIFAVNIMEDIGENI' which translates as '(Property) of the god Fanus Medigenus'. A silver spoon with a 'rat tail' design handle also bears the same inscription.

Notes: His name may translate as 'drink or mead maker' or 'mead begotten'. It seems he was equated with the Roman god Faunus.

Medocius

God

Location: Essex

Evidence: A copper alloy plaque was found at Colchester (Camulodunum) with the inscription 'Deo Marti Medocio Camp-esium et Victorie Alexan-dri Pii Felicis Augusti nos(tr)I donum Lossio Veda de suo posuit nepos Vepogeni Caledowhich' translates as 'To the god Mars Medocius of the Campeses and to the Victory of our Emperor Alexander Pius Felix, Lossio Veda, grandson of Vepogenus, a Caledonian, set up this gift from his own resources.'

Notes: Medocius was it seems, a combination of the Roman god Mars and a local deity, Medocius, perhaps a god of war.

Mogons

God

Location: Cumbria, North Yorkshire, Northumberland

Evidence: A red sandstone altar was found at Old Penrith (Voreda) with the inscription 'Deo

Mog(on)ti' which translates as 'To the god Mogons.'

A red sandstone altar was found at Netherby (Castra Exploratorum) with the inscription 'Deo

Mogont(i) Vitire san(cto) Ael(ius) [Secund(us)] v(otum) s(olvit) l(ibens) m(erito)' which translates as 'To the holy god Mogons Vitiris, Aelius Secundus willingly and deservedly fulfilled his vow.'

A buff sandstone altar was found at Risingham (Habitancum) with the inscription '[D]eo

Mogonito Cad(...) et N(umini) d(omini) n(ostri) Aug(usti) M(arcus) G(avius(?)) Secundinus

[b(ene)]f(iciarius) co(n)s(ularis) Habita-nci prima stat(ione) pro se et suis posu[it]' which translates as 'To the god Mogons Cad(...) and to the Divinity of our Lord Augustus, Marcus Gavius Secundinus, beneficiarius of the governor, on his first tour of duty at Habitancum, set this up for himself and his own.'

Another buff sandstone altar found at Risingham reads 'Deo Mo(g)uno Cad(...) Inventus do(no) [..] v(otum) s(olvit)' which translates as 'To the god Mogunus Cad(...) (from) Inventus as a gift ... fulfilled his vow.'

A buff sandstone altar was found at Chesterholm (Vindolanda) the inscription reads 'deo Mo-

gunti et genio lo-ci Lupul-uș y(otum) ș(olvit) m̦(erito)' which translates as 'To the god Moguns and the Genius of the Place, Lupulus paid his vow, deservedly.' His name is thought to mean 'the Great One'. Inscriptions are found to him in northern Britain but also across Gaul.

Notes: The name Mogons is usually translated to mean 'the Great one'. Inscriptions with his name can be found across northern Britain and eastern Gaul up to Germany. Variations in the spelling include Mogunos, Mogtus and Mountus. The suggestion has been made that Mogons may have been a title used for several different deities, rather than just one god.

Nantosuelta

Goddess

Location: Nottinghamshire

Evidence: Although it seems this goddess was mainly worshipped in Gaul, a relief was uncovered in East Stoke, Nottinghamshire that shows a divine couple that have been identified as the god Sucellus and his Gallic consort Nantosuelta.

Notes: Her name may translate as 'she of the winding brook or river' or 'she of the sun-drenched valley', although the Celtic word 'nant' means 'war'. She appears on several sculptures accompanied by a crow who sits on a round hut.

Nemetona
Goddess
Location: Somerset

Evidence: An oolite altar was found at Bath (Aquae Sulis) bearing the inscription 'Peregrinus Secundi fil(ius) civis Trever Loucetio Marti et Nemetona v(otum) s(olvit) l(ibens) m(erito)' which translates as 'Peregrinus, son of Secundus, a Treveran, to Loucetius Mars and Nemetona willingly and deservedly fulfilled his vow.' Mars Loucetius and Nemetona were sometimes worshipped together.

Notes: Her name translates as 'goddess of the sacred grove' from the Gaulish word 'nemeton' meaning 'sacred grove or sanctuary'.

Nerthus
Goddess
Location: England

Evidence: The Roman historian, Tacticus writes:

> 'The Reudigni, Aviones, Anglii, Varini, Eudoses, Saurines, and Nuitones] share a common worship of Nerthus, or Mother Earth. They believe that she takes part in human affairs, riding in a chariot among her people. On an island of the sea stands an inviolate grove, in which, veiled with a cloth, is a chariot that none but the priest may touch. The priest can feel the presence of the goddess in this holy of holies and attends her with the deepest reverence as

her chariot is drawn along by cows. Then follow days of rejoicing and merrymaking in every place that she condescends to visit and sojourn in. No one goes to war, no one takes up arms; every iron object is locked away. Then, and then only, are peace and quiet known and welcomed, until the goddess, when she has had enough of the society of men, is restored to her sacred precinct by the priest. After that, the chariot, the vestments, and (believe it if you will) the goddess herself, are cleansed in a secluded lake. This service is performed by slaves who are immediately afterwards drowned in the lake. Thus mystery begets terror and a pious reluctance to ask what that sight can be which is seen only by men doomed to die.'

The practices that he describes have been proved to be correct in archaeological finds.

Notes: The Roman historian, Tacticus writes about Nerthus as a Terra Mater, or Earth Mother goddess. He also goes on to describe her sacred animal as the boar. She seems to have been brought over to England by the Germanic people. Her name derives from the Proto Germanic word 'Nerthuz' which translates as 'strong, vigorous, healthy' or the Celtic 'nert' meaning 'force, strength'.

Nodens
God
Location: Gloucestershire, Lancashire

Evidence: A lead plate was uncovered at Lydney Park, Gloucestershire with the inscription 'Devo Nodenti Silvianus anilum perdedit demediam partem donavit Nodenti inter quibus nomen Seniciani nollis petmittas sanita-tem donec perfera(t) usque templum [No-] dentis Rediviva' which translates as 'To the god Nodens: Silvianus has lost his ring and given half (its value) to Nodens. Among those who are called Senicianus do not allow health until he brings it to the temple of Nodens. (This curse) comes into force again.'

A statuette was found at Cockersand Moss, the inscription reads 'Deo Marti Nodonti Aur-elius [. .]cinus sig(illum)' and translates as 'To the god Mars Nodons, Aurelius [...]cinus (set up) this statuette.'

A statuette was found at Cockersand Moss with the inscription 'D(eo) M(arti) N(odonti) Lucianus colleg(ae) Aprili Viato-ris v(otum) s(olvit)' which translates as 'To the god Mars Nodons, Lucianus fulfilled the vow of his colleague, Aprilius Viator.'

A bronze plate was found at Lydney Park with a pentagon shape gable top and featuring a dog image. The inscription reads 'Pectillus votum quod promissit deo Nudente M(arti) dedit' which translates as 'Pectillus gave to the god Nudens Mars the votive offering which he had promised.'

A bronze plate with a nail hole at the top was found at Lydney Park with the inscription 'D(eo) M(arti) Nodonti Flavius Blandinus armature v(otum) s(olvit) l(ibens) m(erito)' which translates as 'To the god Mars Nodons, Flavius Blandinus, weapon-instructor, gladly and deservedly fulfilled his vow.' Lydney Park Temple was dedicated to Nodens Mars (Templvm Marti Nodentis).

Thousands of offerings have been uncovered including a great many coins, nine dog representations and hundreds of pins and bracelets. Mosaics and reliefs depict sea monsters, fish, fishermen and tritons.

Notes: Nodens seems to have been a god of healing and hunting and connected to the ocean. The site at Lydney Park is believed to have been a temple of healing.

Ocelus
God
Location: Cumbria

Evidence: A red sandstone dedication slab was found at Carlisle

(Luguvalium) with the inscription 'Deo Marti Ocelo et Numini imp(eratoris) Alexandri Aug(usti) et Iul(iae) M[ama]eae [ma] tr(i) castr(orum) [et senatus et patr(iae) et toti] domui [divinae ..]' which translates as 'To the god Mars Ocelus and to the Divinity of the Emperor Alexander Augustus, and to Julia Mamaea, mother of the army and senate and country, and to the whole Divine House.' Two other inscriptions mentioning Ocelus have also been found in Wales where he is referred to as Mars Ocelus and Ocelus Vellaunus.

Notes: Ocelus is thought to have been a god of the Silures tribe. The Romans equated him to their god Mars.

Olludius
God
Location: Gloucestershire

Evidence: An oolite relief was found at Customs Scrubs, Bisley in Gloucester. The relief depicts a god wearing a long tunic, cloak and boots holding a patera and a cornucopia. The inscription reads 'Marti Olludio' which translates as 'To Mars Olludius'.

Notes: The Romans linked him to their god Mars so he may have been a war god, however, in the oolite relief image he is also holding a cornucopia which reflects fertility, abundance and harvest. His name may be translated to mean 'great tree'.

Ratis
Goddess
Location: Northumberland, Cumbria

Evidence: A buff sandstone altar was found at Chesters (Cilurnum) fort it bears the inscription 'Dea(e) Rat(i) v(otum) s(olvit) l(ibens)' which translates as 'To the goddess Ratis (someone) willingly fulfilled his vow.'

A buff sandstone altar found at Birdoswald (Banna) with the inscription 'D(e)ae

Rati votu-m in perp-etuo' which translates as 'To the goddess Ratis a vow in perpetuity.'

Notes: No other inscriptions or mentions of this goddess have been found. I have seen the suggestion that she was a goddess of the Iron Age hill forts in and around Northumberland.

Rigisamus
God
Location: Somerset

Evidence: A bronze plate with a handle shape and central hole for attaching to a base was found on a villa site at West Coker in Somerset. It has the inscription 'Deo Marti Rigisamo Iventius Sabinus v(otum) s(olvit) l(aetus) l(ibens) m(erito)'. It translates to read 'To Mars Rigisamus, Iventius Sabinus gladly, willingly, and deservedly fulfilled his vow.'

Notes: The name Rigisamus translates to mean 'Most Kingly'. Worshipped as a war deity in Gaul, his following was brought across to England. The Romans equated him to their god Mars.

Rigonemetis
God
Location: Lincolnshire

Evidence: A limestone dedication slab was found at Nettleham. It has a pelta decoration either side (design resembling a shield). The inscription reads 'deo Marti Rigo-nemeti et numini-bus Augustorum Q(uintus) Nerat(ius) Prox{s}i-mus arcum de suo donavit' which translates as 'To the god Mars Rigonemetis and the Divinities of the Emperors, Quintus Neratius Proximus gave (this) arch at his own expense.'

Notes: The name Rigonemetis translates as 'King of the Sacred Grove'.

Rosmerta
Goddess
Location: Somerset, Gloucester

Evidence: A stone tablet relief found at the Roman Baths, Somerset depicts the Roman god Mercury and thought to be the Celtic goddess Rosmerta. The image shows three Genii Cucullati at their feet. A relief showing them both was found in the Shakespeare Inn, Gloucester where Mercury has a cockerel, caduceus and money bag. Here Rosmerta holds a sceptre and a ladle over a wooden bucket. Another stone image shows Rosmerta with another goddess, possibly the Roman goddess Fortuna. They are both wearing fancy headdresses, both holding what seem to be torches, one held upwards the other down.

Notes: Her name translates as 'good provider'. There are several depictions of Rosmerta across Europe, some show her with Mercury others she is alone. Sometimes with the caduceus or a snake twined staff and often carrying purses or vessels. Some images show her with a bucket or vessel, perhaps a cauldron link showing the idea of resurrection, regeneration and life cycles. The belief is made that she pre-existed Mercury in Gaul and been an independent goddess.

Sabrina
Goddess
Location: The River Severn

Evidence: I have included Sabrina here, although her story begins in Wales at the source of the River Severn, the river itself travels many miles from Wales and into England. It flows through Shropshire Worcestershire and Gloucestershire.

The Dictionary of Ancient Geography by Alexander MacBean dated 1773 gives the following information: 'SABRINA, Tacitus' a river of Britain; now the Severn; Sabriana, Ptolemy; the Bristol Channel.'

Tacitus wrote in his Annals, 'the Ostorius established a line of forts along the rivers Sabrina and Antona'. The Sabrina undoubtedly being the River Severn.

There is also a legend of a Welsh water nymph called Hafren. There are many tales and stories of Sabrina being a water nymph and/or water goddess of the River Severn. Geoffrey of Monmouth writes of her in 1136. The poet John Milton wrote a poem about her in 1634.

Notes: The Welsh name for the River Severn is Hafren from the old Welsh, Habren. The name Sabrina is believed to be derived from Habrena/Habrenna the Briton name, which could mean 'fast river'.

Seaxneat/Saxnôt
God
Location: Essex

Evidence: A 9th Century manuscript contains a vow written in the Saxon dialect. It asks that the Devil be renounced along with three gods, Thunaer (Thor), Wôden (Odin) and Saxnôt.

Notes: In the genealogy of the kings of Essex, Seaxneat appears as the song of Wôden. The word 'seax' was a knife or dagger carried by Saxons. The 'neat' part of the name may derive from 'genēat' which means 'companion/associate'. In old Saxon the name would be Sahsnōt. He was thought to be a tribal god of the Saxons serving as a protector, sovereign of the tribe and warrior.

Senua/Senuna

Goddess

Location: Hertfordshire

Evidence: A votive hoard was discovered in 2003 in Hertfordshire, known as the 'Ashwell hoard'. The haul included more than twenty-seven gold and silver objects including jewellery, plaques and a silver figurine of a woman. Believed to have been taken out of a temple during the late 3rd Century and buried. Several of the plaques bear inscriptions to the goddess Senuna. Later excavations also found an inscribed silver base confirming the figurine is that of the goddess Senuna.

Notes: It is thought she may have been a water goddess connected with a sacred spring or a river named Senua.

Setlocenia

Goddess

Location: Cumbria

Evidence: A red sandstone altar was found at Maryport (Alauna) fort bearing the inscription 'Deae Setlo-ceniae Labar-eus Ge(rmanus) v(otum) s(olvit) l(ibens) m(erito)' which translates as 'To the goddess Setlocenia Labareus, a German, willingly and deservedly fulfilled his vow.'

Notes: Her name translates as 'long life'. The Celtic river name 'Labara' translates as 'the babbler'.

Sucellus/Sucellos

God

Location: York, Nottinghamshire, Gloucestershire, Surrey

Evidence: A silver finger ring was found at York bearing his name. He seems to have been revered at Thorpe in Nottinghamshire where a relief showing a god thought to be Sucellus and a goddess, perhaps his consort Nantosuelta was found. A relief showing a figure holding a hammer was discovered in Chedworth in Gloucestershire and another in Farley Health Temple in Surrey. It is thought both of these finds represent the god Sucellus. Statues of Sucellus have been found in Europe showing him wearing Gallic clothing and carrying a hammer or sometimes a drinking vessel. In some images he is shown wearing a lion or wolf skin on his head.

Notes: He hails from Gaul and came across to England with the Belgae tribe or with the Romans. His name translates as 'good striker'. He is often equated with the Roman god Silvanus.

Sulis

Goddess

Location: Bath

Evidence: A great number of altars, dedications and curse tablets have been found in Bath along with a large temple dedicated to her.

An oolite altar was found at Bath (Aquae Sulis) built into a wall in York Street opposite the Roman Baths. The inscription reads 'Q(uintus) Pompeius Anicetus Suli which' translates as 'Quintus Pompeius Anicetus to Sulis'.

An imported white marble slab fragment was found near the Baths bearing the inscription 'Deae S[uli] Ti(berius) Cl(audius) T[i(beri) fil(ius)] Sollem[nis] [..]' which translates as 'To the goddess Sulis Tiberius Claudius Sollemnis, son of Tiberius, ...'.

An oolite altar was found near the spring of the hot bath bearing the inscription 'Deae

Suli Mi-nervae Sulinus Matu-ri fil(ius) v(otum) s(olvit) l(ibens) m(erito)' which translates as 'To the goddess Sulis Minerva Sulinus, son of Maturus, willingly and deservedly fulfilled his vow.'

An oolitic limestone statue base was found underneath the Pump Room at Bath (Aquae Sulis) with the inscription 'deae Suli L(ucius) Marcius Memor harusp(ex) d(ono) d(edit)' which translates as 'To the goddess Sulis, Lucius Marcius Memor, soothsayer, gave (this) as a gift.' This one is particularly interesting as 'harusp(ex)' indicates a professional divination reader, one who inspects the entrails (human or animal?) to interpret the will of the Gods.

An oolite dedication stone was found near the Great Bath with the inscription 'Priscus Touti f(ilius) lapidariu[s] cives Car[nu-] tenus Su[li] deae v(otum) [s(olvit) l(ibens) m(erito)]' which translates as 'Priscus, son of Toutius, stonemason, a tribesman of the Carnutes, to the goddess Sulis willingly and deservedly fulfilled his vow.'

An oolite altar was found on the site of the Pump Room which reads 'Deae Suli [p]ro salute et [i]ncolumitate Aufidi Maximi (centurio) leg(ionis) VI Vic(tricis) M(arcus) Aufidius Lemnus libertus v(otum) s(olvit) l(ibens) m(erito)' and translates as 'To the goddess Sulis for the welfare and safety of Aufidius Maximus, centurion of the Sixth Legion Victrix, Marcus Aufidius Lemnus, his freedman, willingly and deservedly fulfilled his vow.'

An oolite altar was found at Bath although badly pitted and weathered, the inscription can be made out as 'Dea[e] Suli [o] b s[alutem] sac(rum) G(ai) Iav[oleni Sa]tur[n-] [al]is [...] [i]m[a] g[in]n(iferi) leg(ionis) II Aug(ustae) L(ucius) Manius Dionisias libe(r)t(us) v(otum) s(olvit) l(ibens) m(erito)' and translates as 'To the goddess Sulis on behalf of the welfare of Gaius Javolenus

Saturnalis, ... imaginifer of the Second Legion Augusta, Lucius Manius Dionisias, his freedman, willingly and deservedly fulfilled his vow.' An 'imaginifer' was the bearer of a standard with the Emperor's portrait.

An oolite altar was found on the site of the Pump Room with the inscription '[D]eae Sulipro salute et incolumita-[te] Mar(ci) Aufid[i] [M]aximi (centurio) leg(ionis) VI Vic(tricis) [A]ufidius Eu-tuches leb(ertus) v(otum) s(olvit) l(ibens) m(erito)' and translates as 'To the goddess Sulis for the welfare and safety of Marcus Aufidius Maximus, centurion of the Sixth Legion Victrix, Aufidius Eutuches, his freedman, willingly and deservedly fulfilled his vow.'

An oolite tombstone was found 800m north east from the Roman Baths with the inscription 'D(is) M(anibus) G(aius) Calpurnius [R]eceptus sacer-dos deae Su-lis vix(it) an(nos) LXXV Calpurnia Trifo-sa l[i]bert(a) coniunx f(aciendum) c(uravit)' which translates as 'o the spirits of the departed; Gaius Calpurnius Receptus, priest of the goddess Sulis, lived 75 years; Calpurnia Trifosa, his freedwoman (and) wife, had this set up.'

One hundred and thirty curse tablets were found that had been thrown into the spring all requests made to the goddess Sulis. Each one was made from sheets of lead or pewter, and most were rolled up before being thrown in. All of them seem to be requesting return of stolen items, asking for revenge or the righting of wrongs. Most of them involved what would seem to be today small items such as a stolen towel. Most of the wording is in Latin but two are in an unknown language thought to be Celtic, possibly Brythonic.

Notes: Sulis was worshipped during the Roman times, they equated her to their goddess Minerva. But it seems she was a local goddess long before then. Her name could be from the Proto-Indo-European word for sun or the Gaelic word for eye or hole. Meaning her name is 'goddess of the eye or the gap' which could refer to the healing spring water.

Suleviae

Goddesses

Location: Somerset, Gloucestershire, County Durham, Essex

Evidence: An oolitic limestone altar was found at Cirencester (Corinium Dobunnorum), Gloucestershire, although the base and lower part are broken away it has the inscription 'Sulevis [P]rimus [...]IIAS [...]' which translates as 'To the Suleviae, Primus ...'.

A buff sandstone altar was found at Binchester, Co. Durham with the inscription 'Sul[e(?)]vi[s(?)] [ala] Vett[on(um)] CANN v(otum) s(olvit) l(ibens) m(erito)' which translates as 'To the Suleviae the Cavalry Regiment of Vettonians ... willingly and deservedly fulfilled its vow.'

An oolitic limestone altar was found at Cirencester with the inscription 'Sule(v)is Sulinus Bruceti (filius) v(otum) s(olvit) l(ibens) m(erito)' which translates as 'To the Suleviae, Sulinus, son of Brucetus, willingly and deservedly fulfilled his vow.'

An oolite statue base was found Bath (Aquae Sulis) with the inscription 'Sulevis Sulinus

Sculptor Bruceti f(ilius) sacrum f(ecit) l(ibens) m(erito)' which translates as 'To the Suleviae Sulinus, a sculptor, son of Brucetus, gladly and deservedly made this offering.'.

A green sandstone base was found at Colchester (Camulodunum) with the inscription 'Matribus

Sulevis Similis Atti f(ilius) ci(vis) Cant(iacus) v(otum) l(ibens) s(olvit)' which translates as 'To the Mother Goddesses Suleviae, Similis, son of Attus, a tribesman of the Cantiaci, willingly fulfilled his vow.'

Inscriptions can be found across Great Britain and parts of Europe.

Notes: The name translates as 'good guides' or 'good rulers'. The general consensus seems to be they are mother goddesses, some suggest sisters. They are guardians of the house and home.

Toutatis/Teutatis/Teutates
God
Location: Herefordshire, Cumbria, Lincolnshire and other parts of England

Evidence: A silver votive plaque was found at Barkway, Herefordshire with the inscription 'Marti Toutati Ti(berius) Claudius Primus Attii liber(tus) v(otum) s(olvit) l(ibens) m(erito)' which translates as 'To Mars Toutatis, Tiberius Claudius Primus, freedman of Attius, willingly and deservedly fulfilled his vow.'

A buff sandstone altar was found in Cumbria with the inscription 'I(ovi) O(ptimo) M(aximo) et Riocalat(i) [To]utat(i) M-[ar(ti)] Cocid(i)o [vo]to feci-[t] Vita-[lis]' which translates as 'To Jupiter, Best and Greatest, and to Riocalatis, Toutatis, and Mars Cocidius in fulfilment of a vow Vitalis made (this altar).'

A silver ring found in Lincolnshire bears the inscription 'TOT'.

The Roman poet Lucan in the 1st Century CE referred to Teutates as a Gaulish god who received human sacrifice along with fellow Gaulish gods Taranis and Esus. In the 10th Century CE in the Commenta Berensia a description is given showing the victim for Teutates sacrifices was drowned in a kettle. Taranis' victims were burned in a wooden cask and Esus' were hung on a tree.

Notes: Equated to the Roman god Mars, the Romans referred to him as Teutates. He came across from Gaul but worship of him has been found across England. His name may derive from the Gaulish word 'teuta' meaning 'tribe' or 'people'.

Tridam/us

God

Location: Herefordshire

Evidence: A sandstone altar which had been adapted and trimmed to use as a stoup was found in Michaelchurch, Herefordshire (note, this is not a Roman site or near one). The inscription reads 'Deo Tridam(...) Bellicus don-avit ara[m]' and translates as 'To the god Tridam(...) Bellicus presented this altar.'

Notes: His name may mean 'triple cattle'. There isn't anything else known about this god that I could find.

Vanauns/Vanauntus

God

Location: Cumbria

Evidence: A red sandstone altar was found at Castlesteads (Camboglanna) in Cumbria. It bears the inscription 'N(umini) Aug(usti) deo Vana-unti Aurel(ius) Armiger dec(urio) princ(eps)' which translates as 'To the Divinities of the Emperor (and) to the god Vanauns, Aurelius Armiger, decurio princeps, (set this up).' 'Decurio' is a military officer commanding a 'Princeps' is a centurion acting-commander of a detachment.

Notes: Seemingly worshipped by the Tungrians (from Gaul), there is no mention or reference to this god elsewhere.

Verbeia

Goddess

Location: Yorkshire

Evidence: A gritstone altar was found at Ilkley in Yorkshire decorated with a patera (dish) and a jug. The inscription reads 'Verbeiae sacrum Clodius Fronto praef(ectus) coh(ortis) II Lingon(um)' which translates as 'Sacred to Verbeia: Clodius Fronto, prefect of the Second Cohort of Lingonians (set this up)'. A further stone found on the site shows a female figure wearing a pleated robe and holding two long wavy objects, possibly serpents. A similar stone image was found in Dijon.

Notes: Lingones were a tribe who originated in France, some of them were recruited and stationed at the Roman fort in Ilkley. The name Verbeia was the name of the Roman fort that the altar was found in. It has been suggested the two 'snakes' she holds represent the two streams that flowed either side of the fort into the river Wharfe. A further find in the area has been named the 'Swastika Stone'. It is one of the many pieces of 'cup ring' art found in England, Scotland and across Europe. This particular Swastika Stone was found on Ilkley Moor and is thought to have been carved by the Lingones, who may well have erected the Verbeia altar as well.

Vernostonus
God
Location: County Durham

Evidence: A buff sandstone altar was found at Ebchester (Vindomora) in County Durham with the inscription 'Deo Verno-stono Cocidi-o Viri[l]is Ger(manus) v(otum) s(olvit) l(ibens). It translates as 'To the god Vernostonus Cocidius, Virilis, a German, willingly fulfilled his vow'.

Notes: His name may be linked to alder trees, 'verno' meaning 'alder'.

Vinotonus

God

Location: County Durham,

Evidence: Several items have been found at found at Bowes (Lavatrae) in County Durham.

A sandstone altar with the left side intact but the right side has been cut away. The inscription reads '[Deo] V[inotono]' which translates as 'To the god Vinotonus [...]'.

A millstone grit altar was also found, although worn and weathered, the inscription reads '[Deo] Vinotono Silvano Iul(ius) Secundus (centurio) coh(ortis) I Thrac(um) v(otum) s(olvit) l(aetus) l(ibens) m(erito)' which translates as 'To the god Vinotonus Silvanus, Julius Secundus, centurion of the First Cohort of Thracians, gladly, willingly, and deservedly fulfilled his vow.'

A sandstone altar decorated with a jug, a patera (dish) and a ram's head handle bearing the inscription 'Deo Vin-otono L(ucius) Caesius Frontinus pr-aef(ectus) coh(ortis) I Thrac(um) domo Parma v(otum) s(olvit) l(aetus) l(ibens) m(erito)' which translates as 'To the god Vinotonus, Lucius Caesius Frontinus, prefect of the First Cohort of Thracians, from Parma, gladly, willingly and deservedly fulfilled his vow'.

A buff sandstone altar bearing the inscription 'deo Vino-tono Silva-no Aug(usto) T(itus) [?O]rbius Pri-[?sci]nus pr-[aef] (ectus) [coh(ortis) I Thrac(um)] [v(otum) s(olvit) l(aetus) l(ibens) m(erito)]' which translates as 'To the god Vinotonus Silvanus Augustus, Titus Orbius Priscinus, prefect [of the First Cohort of Thracians, gladly, willingly, and deservedly fulfilled his vow].'

Notes: In one of the inscriptions he is equated to the Roman god Silvanus. His name could be translated to mean 'God of the vines'.

Viridios

God

Location: Lincolnshire

Evidence: An oolitic limestone partial dedication slab was found at Ancaster, Lincolnshire. The inscription reads 'deo Viridio Trenico arcum fecit de șuo don(avit)' which translates as 'For the god Viridius, Trenico made (this) arch and gave it from his own resources.'

A limestone slab fragment was found at Ancaster with the inscription 'deo V(i)rid[io] sanct[o ...] [...]' which translates as 'To the holy god Viridius...'.

The torso of a statue was also found in the same location which may have represented him.

Notes: His name derives from Gallic and could mean 'vigorous'.

Vitiris

God

Location: County Durham, Northumberland, Yorkshire

Evidence: Several altars have been found dedicated to Vitiris some decorated with a serpent and a boar. Here are just some of them:

A buff sandstone was found at Ebchester (Vindomora) with the inscription 'Deo Vitiri I [ ] IT [...]' which translates as 'to the god Vitiris'.

A buff sandstone altar was found at Lanchester (Longovicium) with the inscription 'Deo Vit(iri)' which translates as 'To the god Vitiris'.

A buff sandstone altar was found at Corbridge (Coria/Corstopitum) with the inscription 'Vit(iri) M-iti(us(?))' which translates as 'To Vitiris Mitius (set this up).

A buff sandstone altar was found at Carvoran (Magnis) with

the inscription 'Deo Vitiri Milus et Aurides v(otum) s(olverunt) l(ibentes) m(erito)'. This translates as 'To the god Vitiris Milus and Aurides willingly and deservedly fulfilled their vow.'

A buff sandstone altar was found at Chesters (Cilurnum) with the inscription 'Deo sanc-to Vitiri Tertulus v(otum) s(olvit) l(ibens) m(erito)' which translates as 'To the holy god Vitiris, Tertulus willingly and deservedly fulfilled his vow.'

A buff sandstone altar was found at Chester-le-Street (Concangium) in a Roman well with the inscription 'To the god Vitiris Duihno fulfilled his vow.'

A red sandstone altar was found at Netherby (Castra Exploratorum) with the inscription 'Deo Mogont(i) Vitire san(cto) Ael(ius) [Secund(us)] v(otum) s(olvit) l(ibens) m(erito)' which translates as 'To the holy god Mogons Vitiris, Aelius Secundus willingly and deservedly fulfilled his vow.'

A partial buff sandstone altar was found at Vindolanda with the inscription 'Deo Vi-[tiri] [...]' which translates as 'To the god Vitiris'.

A buff sandstone altar was found at South Shields (Arbeia) although the front is blackened perhaps by fire you can read the inscription 'Deo ⌜ sancto⌝ Vitiri CRN d(edit)' which translates as 'To the holy god Vitiris... gave (this)'.

Notes: He was obviously an important deity. The general consensus is that the name derives from the Latin 'veteris' which means 'the Old One'.

Weland/Weyland/Wayland

God

Location: Oxfordshire

Evidence: References to this smith god mostly come from folklore and stories. His story can be found in the Völundarkvida, a 13th century Icelandic Edda. You will also find mention of him in the Anglo-Saxon poems Waldere and Deor from Beowulf.

Alfred the Great also makes reference to him in the 9th Century Boëthius. The connection we are concerned with links him to a stone burial chamber near White Horse Hill in Oxfordshire, known as Wayland's Smithy. The site is a Neolithic long barrow and legend says it was once the home of the Saxon god of metal working, Wayland.

Notes: Known as the lame Saxon blacksmith god he is equated to Wieland in Germany and the Norse Volundr.

Making a Connection

If you feel drawn to any of these deities, or any gods or goddesses from around the world for that matter, there are some simple ways to connect. If you live near any of the places they are associated with or happen to be visiting the area I would encourage you to make a visit. Once on a site you can try and make a connection with the energy of the land. Sit quietly and breathe slowly in and out, as if you were beginning to meditate. Now open your senses to the land, to the flora and fauna around you and to the ground beneath you. Send out a request to the ancestors, to the deity you want to connect with and see what happens. If at any time you feel uncomfortable or uneasy know that you are in total control and can shut down the connection immediately. Bring up your psychic shields and walk away. Hopefully you make a positive contact, be open to what comes to you, listen and pay attention to any sights, sounds and feelings. Once you are done, give thanks and, if possible, leave an offering, make sure it is biodegradable.

- Learn all you can about the deity and the landscape, do some research, read up on the history of the place and the god or goddess. Knowledge is power!
- Set up an altar dedicated to the deity you want to connect with, it doesn't need to be a grand affair. Include a

photograph of the area they are associated with and any flowers, herbs or items you feel need to be there.

- Meditate to connect with them. Write out some notes first to set a scene, using photographs or memories if you have visited, describe the landscape to walk through in your meditation. Put out a request for the deity to join you there.

- Create an incense or essential oil blend that you believe represents the deity, use it when you are meditating or sitting at your altar.

- Write and perform a ritual to draw upon the energy of the deity.

- Create a poppet or spirit doll from felt or other craft materials to represent the deity.

- Make a set of mala or prayer beads to use when meditating with the deity, include beads that you feel correspond to them and their energies.

- Mandalas are lovely ways to connect. Create an image from natural items, crystals or any small objects you feel are right, to help you contact and/or honour deity.

- One of my favourite ways to make a connection particularly with a specific area is to research the local foods and recipes. There are a lot of old and familiar recipes connected with particular areas of England (and across the globe). I like to seek out recipes that have those connections and make them, I find it helps me align with the energies of the area and I get something yummy to eat too, it's a win win situation!

Meet the Deities

Here I have included some examples of how I work with these deities. This may help you connect with them but also give you a template for working with others. Because there is so little information about most of them, I have included my own personal correspondences and symbols, things I believe work with them. You may have different thoughts. Trust your intuition.

Belisama

Belisama History/myths/origins

Belisama is a Gaulish goddess, and her name translates as 'the brightest one' or 'the most powerful'. A lot of information about her has been lost in the mists of time but it is believed that she was a popular goddess. Sometimes seen as the consort to the god, Belenus. She is a goddess of fire and the power of light within the sun and the moon. The Romans took Belisama and incorporated her into their own goddess, Minerva. The ancient writer Ptolemy wrote about 'the Belisama estuary' being the river Ribble in Lancashire, England. Her cult was well known in France, worshipping their goddess particularly on the battlefield for bravery and valour.

Her name rarely appears in inscriptions. However, two examples have been found that mention her name. Both were found in old Gaulish lands. A dedication found in Lyon, France (home to the Consoranni tribe), is on an altar. The wording associates her with the Roman goddess Minerva and translates as "Sacred to Minerva Belisama, offered this monument in accomplishment of his vow".

The other inscription was found in Vaison-la-Romaine, the chief city of the Vocontii tribe. This one translates to read "Segomaros son of Villu, citizen of Nimes, offered this sacred enclosure to Belesama". The names Segomaros and Villoneos are Celtic. Segomaros offers the goddess a nemeton, which translates as 'sacred enclosure' or 'sanctuary'. The nemeton was a sacred place reserved for worship to deity where only initiates of the cult were allowed.

Researchers have confirmed that there is no doubt Belisama comes from the Celtic culture.

The River Ribble runs through North Yorkshire and Lancashire in Northern England. It starts close to the Ribblehead Viaduct in North Yorkshire and is one of the few that start in the Yorkshire Dales and flow westwards towards the sea. The name Ribble may be a Brittonic compound-formation. With translations such as "puddle, pond, upland-stream" (Welsh pwll). And "great". Ribble may once have been known as 'Bremetonā', underlying the name Bremetenacum, the Roman fort at Ribchester. Involved here is the Brittonic root 'breμ', meaning "roaring". In Roman times it seems the river may also have been known as the Belisama.

Area associated with
River Ribble, Lancashire
Various sites in France
Milan, Italy

Other names/spellings
Minervae Belissimae
Belisama Minerva
Beleymas
Belleme

Correspondences

Element:	Fire, Water
Colours:	Red, orange, blue
Herbs and Plants:	Anemone, bay, betony, buttercup, celandine, clove, copal, dittany, flax, garlic, ginger, heliotrope, juniper, marigold, mustard, nettle, oak, rosemary, sunflower, tobacco, woodruff
Stones:	Agate, amber, carnelian, citrine, garnet, jasper, black obsidian, pyrite, quartz, sunstone, tiger's eye
Animals:	Owl, river dwelling animals
Symbols:	Flames, sun, flowing water, full moon
Places:	Groves, rivers, around fires
Suggested offerings:	Dried herbs, ashes, yellow flowers

Call upon her for
Bravery
Valour
Strength
Inspiration
Strategy
Creativity

Protection
Wisdom
Changes

Belisama Meditation

Make yourself comfortable in a place where you won't be disturbed. Close your eyes and begin to focus on your breathing. Take deep breaths in...and out.

As the world around you dissipates you find yourself standing on a riverbank, the sun is shining, and the air is warm.

Turn and look at your surroundings, the river rushing past you on one side and on the other...a structure. It looks like a temple of some sort, so you walk towards it.

There is an open doorway, and you can smell the sweet musky scent of incense drifting on the air from inside.

Step through the doorway...

Inside is space, lots of empty space. Apart from an what looks like an altar at one end of the room.

Head towards the altar and take a look.

There are candles and bowls of dried herbs and fruit laid out.

The incense you smelt as you came in is burning in a large dish set to one side.

Also, on the altar are slips of parchment and a quill pen beside a bottle of ink.

As you are investigating all the items you hear someone enter the room, you turn...

A beautiful woman stands before you, she looks strong and powerful but has a kindness in her eyes.

She beckons you to sit down in front of the altar with her.

You talk, ask questions, listen to the answers.

She encourages you to write a petition on the parchment, picking up the quill pen you did it in the ink and write...something you desire or want to let go of, perhaps an inspiration required.

Once you have written your petition you light the corner of the paper one the flame from a candle and drop it into a large stone dish.

Watch the flame and the smoke as it burns.

The woman hugs you and then hands you a small pebble with an image drawn on, you take it with thanks.

She bids you farewell.

Head back out of the room and through the doorway to where you began beside the river.

Slowly and gently come back to the here and now, wriggle your fingers and toes and open your eyes. Have a drink and something to eat and write down the message that you were given.

Belisama Ritual

Belisama brings the fiery energy of the sun for inspiration. This ritual draws upon that to help you open your creative avenues.

You will need:

A red candle
An orange candle
A yellow candle
Quarter candles (optional)
Central candle

Cast your circle by walking deosil (clockwise) around your space three times, visualise a protective bubble surrounding you.

Face each direction in turn to call in the elements; you could even place a lighted candle at each quarter:

I call to the East, the element of air
Chill winds and icy blasts
The intellect carried by the birds of the sea
I welcome you

I call to the South, the element of fire
Island volcanoes and shoreline fires
Bring your passion and energy
I welcome you

I call to the West, the element of water
The oceans, the rivers
The intuition of the wells and springs
I welcome you

I call to the North, the element of Earth
The rocks, the mountains
The stability of the earth
I welcome you

Call upon the Goddess Belisama:

Goddess Belisama, she of the powerful light
I invite you to join me in this rite, to lend your energy, inspiration
and creativity.
I welcome you

Now light your central candle. Set the three coloured candles in front of you. Light the red candle saying:

Belisama, I ask that you fill me with inspiration.

Light the orange candle saying:

Belisama, I ask that you fill me with creativity.

Light the yellow candle saying:

Belisama, I ask that you fill me with energy.

Now sit quietly focusing on the candle flames. Draw in the energy from the flames but also watch to see for any images or movement. Do you feel drawn to one coloured candle in particular? Listen also for any messages. Take your time and allow the energy to fill your body and mind.

When you are ready snuff out each of the three candles saying:

Dearest Belisama, I take the flame and hold onto the energy, allowing it to continue to flow through me.

Now face the centre and thank Belisama for joining you and bid her farewell and snuff out the central candle:

To the inspiring goddess Belisama, with my thanks for your energy in this rite today. I bid you farewell.

Turn to each direction and thank them for lending their energies to the rite and bid them hail and farewell:

I thank the element of water and the direction of West for your presence here today.
I bid you farewell.
I thank the element of fire and the direction of South for your presence here today.
I bid you farewell.
I thank the element of air and the direction of East for your presence here today.

I bid you farewell.
I thank the element of earth and the direction of North for your presence here today.
I bid you farewell.

Walk widdershins (anti clockwise) around the circle stating out loud:

This circle is open but never broken, blessed be.

Recipe – Chorley Cakes

Buttery pastry filled with sweet currants, these cakes hail from Chorley in Lancashire, England.

For the pastry:

300g/10 oz plain/all-purpose flour
1 teaspoon baking powder
25g/1 oz caster sugar
180g/6 oz butter
80ml/3 fl oz milk

For the filling:

200g/7 oz currants, sultanas or mixed dried fruit
50g/2 oz soft light brown sugar
50g/2 oz melted butter

To make the pastry, pop the flour, baking powder and sugar into a bowl. Add the butter and rub in until it resembles breadcrumbs. Stir in the milk and mix to bring together as a soft dough. Add a little more milk if necessary. Wrap in cling film and pop in the fridge for half an hour.

For the filling mix the currants, sugar and melted butter

together and set aside.

Preheat your oven to 190C/375F/Gas 5.

Roll out the pastry.

You can make 8 large cakes or 12 smaller ones (both are shown in the image)

For large Chorley cakes – use a large cookie cutter (14cm) to stamp out 8 rounds.

For smaller Chorley cakes – use a small (7cm) cookie cutter to stamp out 24 rounds (a bottom and top for each cake).

Place a spoonful of the filling in the centre of the pastry circle and dampen the edges with a little water.

For the large cakes fold the pastry over to enclose the filling, turn over and lightly flatten.

For the smaller cakes place a circle of pastry over the top of each one and seal the edges.

Brush the tops of the cakes with a little milk or beaten egg if you wish.

Using a knife make a small cut in the top of each cake.

Bake in the oven for 25-30 minutes until golden brown.

Vegan option:

Replace the butter in the pastry with half vegan butter, half vegetable shortening.

For the filling replace with vegan butter.

Gluten free option:

Replace the flour with a GF flour blend. I find it also helps to replace half the butter with vegetable shortening.

The Three Mothers/Matres

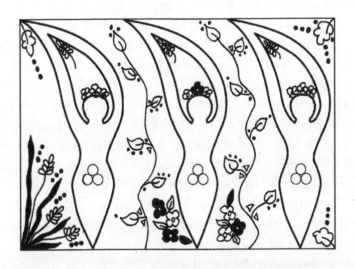

The Three Mothers/Matres History/Myths/Origins

The Three Mothers are based on the findings from archaeological digs in and around Ashcroft in Cirencester, Gloucestershire in an area referred to as The Cotswolds. In 1899 a carved limestone relief depicting three goddesses sitting down holding baskets of bread and fruits was discovered, dating back to the 2nd or 3rd Century CE. The three mothers here are wearing knee length clothing and cloaks, two of them appear to have headdresses, which could indicate marriage. Perhaps the baskets of produce represent abundance and a connection or correspondence to Mother Nature.

The number of items discovered at this site and others locally also indicates there was a large temple or shrine dedicated to the mothers or Matres. It has been suggested that a cult in and around Roman Corinium (Cirencester) worshipped the Matres. The Matres do seem to be important to this specific area but altars and inscriptions to mother goddesses can be found across Britain and Northern Europe.

Evidence of a Cult of Matres has been found in Gaul (modern France) dating back to the 1st century CE. It seems that the idea of the Matres cult may have been brought into Britain from Europe.

They may have been seen as household deities and shrines would have been kept inside each home with offerings made for protection and abundance.

The local name in Cirencester for the Matres may have been the 'Suleviae'. Based on inscriptions found including the one on an altar recovered at Ashcroft in 1899. The inscription refers to the Mothers of Suleviae. However, when translating 'Matres Suleviae' it may derive from the Proto Celtic 'su' or 'good' or the Proto Celtic 'sawol' or 'sun'. Meaning Mothers of Good or Mothers of the Sun. The name may also translate as 'good guides' or 'good rulers'.

Inscriptions can be found across Great Britain and parts of Europe. The consensus seems to be they are mother goddesses, some suggest sisters. They are guardians of the house and home.

Another item recovered from a site in Cirencester in 1964 is a relief showing the mother goddess sitting beside the Genii Cucullati or the Hooded Spirits. No one knows what the images actually mean but the suggestion has been made that the spirits represent fertility and protection alongside the Matres. The hooded cape or 'cucullus' was very typical of Gauls and Celts and often worn by the upper classes. The Celts also believed the number three to be very significant.

Genii Cucullati seem to appear throughout Celtic Britain and Europe, usually in groups of three, always wearing the cloak or hood. Perhaps to symbolise that they are spirits and usually invisible.

It has been suggested that the spirits bring fertility and protection but also healing as they are often associated with natural spa sites. Sometimes called 'spirits of place', the Latin 'genii loci' or using the Old English word 'landwight'. They have also been identified as possibly being the male counterparts to the three Matres or Matronae.

Another relief showing three Matres, was found in Cirencester. This one showing the centre woman nursing a baby. A further relief found in 1899 shows three mother goddesses dealing with what look like unruly children.

There are a large number of inscriptions made to the Matres or Mothers found across Britain. Usually made in dedications to a particular country, area or specific role such as 'household mothers'.

Area Associated with

Cirencester, England

General Matres worship can be found across Britain and Europe

Other Names/Spellings

Matres

Deae Matronae (Great or Divine Mother Goddess)

Matrones

Nutrices (nursing mothers)

Correspondences

Element:	Earth, water
Colours:	Brown, green, blue
Herbs and Plants:	Birch, blackthorn, borage, buttercup, celandine, chickweed, clover, cornflower, cyclamen, daffodil, daisy, dandelion, dock, elder, feverfew, foxglove, geranium, gorse, grass, hawthorn, hazel, heather, horehound, horsetail, ivy, lavender, lilac, lovage, mistletoe, mugwort, nettle, oak, periwinkle, plantain, poppy, primrose, rose, rowan, rue, self-heal, tansy, thistle, willow, wormwood

Crystals:	Agate, bloodstone, carnelian, garnet, hematite, jasper, labradorite, obsidian (black), pebble, quartz, sunstone
Animals:	Ravens, dogs
Symbols:	Cornucopia, baskets, wheat sheafs, threes
Places:	The home
Suggested offerings:	Flowers, fruit, grains, coins

Call upon them for

Fertility
Protection
Home and hearth
Prosperity
Abundance
Family
Community
Good fortune
Providing

Three Mothers/Matres Meditation

Make yourself comfortable in a place where you won't be disturbed. Close your eyes and focus on your breathing. Deep breaths in...deep breaths out.

As the world around you dissipates you find yourself a busy marketplace.

Voices all around you, chatting and calling out offering their wares.

Livestock and animals of all kinds are being herded past you and through the narrow pathway between the stalls.

Take a look at the vendors around you. Walk to each stall and look.

Talk to the vendors. Smell the produce, pick it up and feel the texture.

Fresh brightly coloured fruit and vegetables piled high.

Spices and herbs in large round baskets loaded onto tables and spreading out across the ground. Which ones can you identify?

Flowers of every colour and shape. Pick some of them up and breathe in the scent.

Hand woven baskets in different shapes, sizes and designs piled high.

Freshly baked bread and cakes in so many varieties. The vendor offers you a small cake to try, you accept with thanks and eat it slowly. It is delicious. What flavours can you identify?

Fabric, clothing and rugs in a myriad of colours and patterns. Pick up some of them and feel the texture of the cloth.

Take in the smells, the sounds and the sights.

It is bustling and buzzing with energy, sound and abundance.

As you walk through the stalls you come to what looks like the centre of the village. A round stone fountain filled with glistening water.

Seated on the wall around the edge are three women.

Mature in years and dressed in layer upon layer of coloured fabric. All with cloaks around their shoulders and two of them have flower circlets on their heads. What do you notice about each of them in particular?

Each woman is holding a woven basket filled with fruit and freshly baked bread.

They talk incessantly to each other, laughing and joking loudly.

The women look up as you approach. One of them gestures for you to sit beside them. She is kind and friendly, so you sit.

Once you are seated you drop your hand into the water of the fountain and feel the chill coldness against your skin.

The women chat quietly with you about general things and then one of the women asks if they can help you with anything.

You find yourself opening up to them. They listen patiently…

And then they reply to you in turn with their thoughts.

Listen carefully.

When they have finished talking to you one of them reaches into

her basket and hands you a gift.
You accept it with thanks. What have you been given? What does it mean to you?
Each woman now stands to give you a warm embracing hug and you thank them and bid your farewell.
Walk back through the market, take another look at any of the stalls that interest you. Look at the produce, talk to the vendors. Take in the sights, the sounds and the smells.
Back to the point where you arrived.
Take a last look back and then at the gift you were given.

Slowly and gently come back to this reality. Open your eyes and wriggle your fingers and toes.

Three Mothers/Matres Ritual
This ritual is done within your house and will bring protection, cleansing, love and abundance to the energy of your home and those within it.

You will need:

> *A small bowl*
> *Jug of water*
> *Salt*
> *Rose petals (fresh or dried)*

Cast your circle by either walking around your property or visualising a circle surrounding your home, then becoming a globe, above and below:

> *I cast this circle round about to keep unwanted spirits out. Inside this circle fill with love, magic energy below and above.*

Call in the elements.

Element of air, blowing in from the east, I invite you to bring intuition and intellect.
Welcome.
Element of fire, raging in from the south, I invite you to bring passion and creativity.
Welcome.
Element of water, flowing in from the west, I invite you to bring cleansing and emotions.
Welcome.
Element of earth, set firmly in the north, I invite you to bring stability and grounding.
Welcome.

Deity:

I call upon the Three Mothers, the Matres, to bring your abundance and home and hearth energy to this rite.
Welcome.

Take your bowl and pour in some water, say:

Water of life, cleansing and purifying. Clear my home from negative energy and that which no longer serves me.

Now add a pinch of salt and say:

Salt of the earth, grounding and stabilising, bring positive energy, stability and good health to our home.

Add a few rose petals to the mix and say:

Beauty of the rose, bring abundance, love and happiness to our home and family.

Give the mix a swirl. Walk around your home and sprinkle a little of the water into the corner of each room, say:

With the energy of the Three Mothers, The Matres, blessings be upon this house and all who reside within.

When you are finished tip any remaining water onto the ground outside. Eat and drink.

Deity:

I thank the Three Mothers, the Matres for your energy today and ask that you keep watch over my home and family. Farewell.

Elements:

To the energy of earth and the direction of north, I thank you. Farewell
To the energy of water and the direction of west, I thank you Farewell
To the energy of fire and the direction of south, I thank you Farewell
To the energy of air and the direction of east, I thank you Farewell

You may wish to leave the circle cast around your home. If not, visualise the circle dissipating into the air:

The circle is open, but not broken.

Recipe – Gloucester Pancakes

Although the name states pancakes and they are cooked on hot griddle or pan, they look and taste more like fluffy flaky scones – delicious with jam or syrup.

170g/6 oz plain/all-purpose flour
85g/3 oz shredded suet or vegetable shortening
1 egg
Pinch of salt
1 level teaspoon baking powder
Few tablespoons milk
Shortening or butter to fry

Mix the flour, baking powder and salt together and rub in the suet. If you are using vegetable shortening it helps to place the shortening in the freezer for half an hour first, so it is easier to grate.

Mix in the egg and enough milk to make a stiff but soft dough, add the milk a tablespoon at a time.

Roll out the dough on a floured surface to a depth of about half an inch, cut into rounds using a 2" cookie cutter (or a glass/cup).

Melt some butter or shortening in a pan or on a griddle and fry the pancakes until golden brown on both sides.

Serve warm with syrup or jam.

They are also nice sliced open and spread with butter.

Sabrina

Sabrina History/myths/origins

Sabrina is a goddess of the River Severn, which begins its journey in Wales, ending up in the sea. Sabrina is thought to be the Romanised version of Havren/Habren which is her original Welsh name, or Habrenna her Briton name.

She is thought to be one of the earliest recorded goddesses of a British river. Mentioned in the 2nd Century as a goddess who rides her chariot through the river with dolphins and salmon swimming along beside her. In the 6th Century when the Brythonic Britons and Anglo Saxons met, the river created a boundary between them. The Saxons called the river Unla. The Saxon word translates as 'misfortune'. Perhaps they tried to cross the river, and many were drowned in the currents and whirlpools. The River Severn frequently floods its banks creating water meadows that cover with shrouds of mist in early morning. Geoffrey of Monmouth writes about her in The History of the Kings of Britain. Brutus of Troy led a band of Trojan exiles to Britain. On arrival they discovered that Britain was full of giants, so they went to battle, slaying them all. The land was then divided into four parts and given to his three sons: Locrine/Locrin (England), Camber (Wales) and Albanact/ Albanactus (Scotland), the fourth part (Cornwall) going to his friend Corineus. After the death of Brutus, Corineus's daughter, Guendolen/Gwendolen was promised to Locrine in marriage. However, before the happy couple were wed, Britain was invaded by the Huns led by Humber.

Locrine was the leader of the battle and in the process captured a princess called Estrildis, who was the daughter of Humber. The Huns were beaten, and Humber killed, falling into a river, which still bears his name to this day. Locrine fell in love with his prisoner. A request was made by Locrine to Corineus to release him from his engagement to Guendolen, but Corineus would not agree. So...Locrine married Guendolen. But he built secret rooms in the basement of his castle to house

Estrildis...tsk tsk naughty boy. Over the next seven years this deception carried on, with Locrine 'going to make offerings to the gods' on a regular basis. His excuse to Guendolen each time he visited his mistress. Estrildis became pregnant during that time and gave birth to a daughter, Havren.

On the death of Corineus, Locrine divorced Guendolen and released Estrildis and Havren from hiding in the basement. Guendolen was obviously unhappy about the whole situation and raised an army to march against Locrine (as you do...) and he was killed in the ensuing battle. Guendolen gave the order to throw Estrildis and Havren into the river that ran through Locrine's kingdom. She named the river after Havren so that the story of Locrine's infidelity would be remembered forever.

And so, the river was named Havren...until the Romans arrived and changed the name, as they liked to do. Renaming it Sabrina, which translates as 'from the boundary'. Monmouth also gives a tale of three water spirit sisters; they meet on the slopes of Plynlimon to create a plan to reach the sea.

The first sister decides to take the direct route, heading west and becoming the river Ystwyth.

The second sister liked to meander, taking her through the hills and valleys, becoming the river Wye.

The third sister (our Sabrina) decided to take her time, travelling 180 miles to reach the sea, taking her through as many towns as possible. She became the River Severn.

The poet Milton also wrote about Sabrina, a water nymph who rescues the Lady from her plight. She is seen as a powerful nymph who hears the plights of women in need.

The river crosses many boundaries and takes the story of the water nymph and creates a goddess.

Area associated with

River Severn – on Plynlimon, close to the Ceredigion/Powys border near Llanidloes, in the Cambrian Mountains of mid Wales. It then flows through Shropshire, Worcestershire and Gloucestershire, with the county towns of Shrewsbury, Worcester and Gloucester on its banks. It is the longest river in Britain.

Other names/spellings

Havren

Habren

Hafren

Habrenna

Severn

Afon Hafren

Correspondences

Element:	Water
Colours:	Blue, green, white
Herbs and Plants:	Water lily, willow, grasses, burdock, chickweed, cleavers, coltsfoot, columbine (aquilegia), comfrey, cowslip, daisy, elder, iris, primrose, geranium, witch hazel, buttercup, betony
Crystals:	Pebbles, agate, amethyst, fluorite, labradorite, lapis lazuli, moonstone, black obsidian, quartz, sodalite, tourmaline
Animals:	Swans, dolphins, salmon
Symbols:	Bull rushes, willow tree
Places:	Rivers, boundaries, where the river meets the sea, mists
Suggested offerings:	Flowers, flower petals

Call upon her for

Protection

Creating boundaries

Wishes

Blessings

Emotions

Movement

Going with the flow

Between the world's connection

Freedom

Self-worth

Sabrina Meditation

Make yourself comfortable in a place where you won't be disturbed. Close your eyes and begin to focus on your breathing. Take deep breaths in...and out.

As the world around you dissipates you find yourself sitting on a grassy bank beside a large river.

It is early morning, just after dawn and the river is shrouded in a light mist.

Look at your surroundings, feel the lush grass beneath you, scattered with bright yellow buttercups.

The river stretches out before you, so wide you can barely see the other side. The water moves quickly heading off into the distance.

The edge of the bank drifts down into the water, blurred by tall rushes and grasses growing up from the mud.

As you sit and watch the water you see something, ripples in the surface of the water. Realising it is salmon swimming along with the current of the water you continue to watch their progress.

The sun is rising, and the mist is starting to clear. As it does you can just make out a figure standing on the riverbank just further along from you.

A woman...she beckons you towards her, so you walk slowly in her direction.

As you reach where she stands, she doesn't say a word, just turns and looks out over the water.

Although she says no words directly, you can hear her voice inside your head. She turns to face the river back from the direction you came in and asks you to do the same.

This is the past, the way you have come.

Then she turns and looks ahead, in the direction the river is travelling.

This is the future, the way you are going.

Then she places her hand on your heart and you hear the words "this is now".

You feel the need to talk, to ask her questions, to share your thoughts. She wants you to know that you have purpose and direction and that you can set boundaries.

Make time for your plans, your future, your dreams. Whilst you can help others, you need to help yourself first.

Talk with her...

When you are finished, she hands you a small pebble with a symbol painted on. Take the gift and thank her.

She turns and seems to literally melt into the ripples of the river.

Take a last look at the river...

Slowly and gently come back to the here and now, wriggle your fingers and toes and open your eyes. Have a drink and something to eat and write down the message that you were given.

Sabrina Ritual

Everyone needs to set boundaries in life so that others don't cross into your space. It is very easy in our busy lives to allow others to overstep, and it can cause quite a lot of issues. This ritual draws on the power of Sabrina to help you set boundaries to look after your own wellbeing.

You will need:

A sheet of paper
A piece of string (biodegradable)
Pencil or pen

Quarter candles (optional)
Central candle

Cast your circle by walking deosil (clockwise) around your space three times, visualise a protective bubble surrounding you. Face each direction in turn to call in the elements; you could even place a lighted candle at each quarter:

I call to the East, the element of air
Chill winds and icy blasts
The intellect carried by the birds of the sea
I welcome you

I call to the South, the element of fire
Island volcanoes and shoreline fires
Bring your passion and energy
I welcome you

I call to the West, the element of water
The oceans, the rivers
The intuition of the wells and springs
I welcome you

I call to the North, the element of Earth
The rocks, the mountains
The stability of the earth
I welcome you

Call upon the Goddess Sabrina:

Sabrina Fair, nymph of the water
I invite you to join me in this rite, to lend your energy, wisdom
and knowledge.
I welcome you

Now light your central candle. Take a sheet of paper and draw a large circle. Now write all the areas of your life that are special to you inside the circle. This might include meditation time, reading a book, taking a bath, any kind of self-care event that you love to do on your own. Next write the areas of your life that you are happy to share with others, outside of the circle. This might include family dinner, going to the shops, cinema trips and any event that you like to do with friends and family.

This is about setting a boundary so that you can have those quiet personal times without the children, pets, friends or family over stepping. When you are ready fold the paper up and tie it with a piece of string (biodegradable). This can then be placed outside to weather and wash away in the rain or thrown into running water. Now face the centre and thank Sabrina for joining you and bid her Hail and Farewell and snuff out the central candle:

To the beautiful goddess Sabrina, with my thanks for your energy in this rite today. I bid you farewell.

Turn to each direction and thank them for lending their energies to the rite and bid them hail and farewell:

I thank the element of water and the direction of West for your presence here today.
I bid you farewell
I thank the element of fire and the direction of South for your presence here today.
I bid you farewell
I thank the element of air and the direction of East for your presence here today.
I bid you farewell
I thank the element of earth and the direction of North for your presence here today.

I bid you farewell

Walk widdershins (anti clockwise) around the circle stating out loud:

This circle is open but never broken, blessed be.

Recipe – Shearing Cake

This recipe was made to feed the shearers at shearing time, also called the Threshing Cake which would have been served to the workers at harvest time. The original recipe would probably have used bacon fat and butter milk. Some recipes include nutmeg and lemon as this one does, other omit those and replace them with mixed peel. At shearing time all the farms in the area would help each other out, moving from each farm in turn to round up and shear the sheep. The host farm was expected to put on food for the workers.

1 lb (500g or 4 cups) plain flour,
1 rounded teaspoon baking powder
225g/8 oz butter
340g/12 oz soft brown sugar
1 tablespoon caraway seeds
grated rind and juice of 1 lemon
1 teaspoon grated nutmeg
300ml/1/2 pint milk
2 eggs
pinch of salt

Rub the butter into the flour sifted with the baking powder. Add the sugar, lemon rind and juice, caraway seeds, nutmeg and a pinch of salt. Slowly pour in the milk, mixing well all the time, and finally add the well beaten eggs. Line a 9-inch cake tin with greased paper and pour in the cake mix. Bake for about 2 hours in a moderate oven 350F (180C) – lowering the heat to 300F (150C) after the first 1/2 hour (30 minutes). If the cake browns too quick, cover the top with greaseproof paper or foil but remove it for the last 1/2 hour (30 minutes) of cooking. When slightly cooled, turn out of the tin and place on a wire rack.

Gluten Free: Replace flour with the equal quantity of oat flour. Increase the milk to 400ml (13.5 fl oz).

An English Ending

Many these English deities have long been forgotten, I am making it my mission to keep their history alive, and I invite you to join me. No matter where you live in the world you can connect with any of these deities. Obviously if you are able to visit the sites then even better, but it isn't essential. What I would recommend you do, is to connect with the energy of the land you live on. Research the history for your own area and get to know the land beneath your feet. You may be surprised what you find.

Reference and Further Reading

For useful information on archaeological finds https://
romaninscriptionsofbritain.org/

For useful information on Roman sites http://www.roman-
britain.co.uk/

A Companion to Roman Britain – edited by Todd, Malcolm
Aspects of the archaeology of the Brigantes by Kenneth J Fairless
Britain BC by Francis Pryor
Comus by John Milton
Ecclesiastical History of the English People by Bede
Gods, Heroes and Kings by Christopher R Fee & David A
    Leeming
Helith, an Anglo-Saxon Pagan Deity by Swain Wodening &
    Gunivortus Goos
Historia Regum Britanniae by Geoffrey of Monmouth
History of Ancient Britain by Neil Oliver
History of Britain by Richard Dargie
Home by Francis Pryor
Pagan Gods and Shrines by Oxford University Committee for
    Archaeology Monographs
Pagan Portals - Gods & Goddesses of Ireland by Morgan Daimler
Pagan Portals - Gods & Goddesses of Wales by Halo Quin
Pagan Portals - Nemetona by Joanna van der Hoeven
Religion in Roman Britain by Martin Henig
Study of the Deposition & Distribution of Copper Alloy Vessels
    in Roman Britain by Lundock, Jason Richard
Sucellus and Nantosuelta in Mediaeval Celtic Mythology by FM
    Heichelheim and J E Housman
Symbol and Image in Celtic Religious Art by Miranda Green
Tacitus, Cornelius. 1948. Germania 40. In The Agricola and

Germania. Translated by Harold Mattingly
The Ancient Paths by Graham Robb
The Anglo-Saxon Charms by Felix Grendon
The Gods of the Celts by Miranda Green
The Isles of the Many Gods by David Rankine & Sorita D'Este
The Lost Gods of England by Brian Bramston
The Old Ways by Robert MacFarlane
Verbeia pdf by Gyrus

The Mythological Cycle of books
The Ulster Cycle of books
The Fionn Cycle of books
The Mabinogion
The Eddas
The Skaldic Verses
The Gododin Poems

Museum, Buxton
Museum, Southampton Sea City
Museum, The British
Museum, Vercovicium Roman, Northumberland

www.academia.edu
www.ancienttexts.org
www.britannica.com
www.curses.csad.ox.ac.uk/index.shtml
www.deomercurio.be/en/silvano.html
www.deomercurio.be/en/suleviis.html
www.dot-domesday.me.uk
www.en-academic.com
www.english-heritage.org.uk
www.heritagedaily.com
www.intarch.ac.uk
www.larhusfyrnsida.com

www.mistshadows.blogspot.com/2019/01/a-new-identification-
of-north-british.html

www.oxfordreference.com

www.romanbaths.co.uk

www.wales.ac.uk (University of Wales)

About the Author

I am a Pagan Witch, working wife and mother who has also been lucky enough to write and have published a fair number of books on the Craft. I love to learn, I love to study and have done so from books, online resources, schools and wonderful mentors over the past thirty years or so and continue to learn every day but have learnt the most from getting outside and doing it. I am High Priestess of the Kitchen Witch Coven and an Elder at the online Kitchen Witch School.

I like to laugh, bake and eat cake...

www.rachelpatterson.co.uk
facebook.com/rachelpattersonbooks

www.kitchenwitchhearth.net
facebook.com/kitchenwitchuk
Email: HQ@kitchenwitchhearth.net

www.youtube.com/user/Kitchenwitchuk
www.instagram.com/racheltansypatterson

My craft is a combination of old religion
Witchcraft, Kitchen Witchery,
Hedge Witchery and folk magic. My heart is
that of a Kitchen Witch.

My craft is a combination of old religion
Witchcraft, Kitchen Witchery,
Hedge Witchery and folk magic. My heart is
that of a Kitchen Witch.

MY BOOKS

Kitchen Witchcraft Series
Spells & Charms
Garden Magic
Crystal Magic
The Element of Earth
The Element of Fire

Pagan Portals
Kitchen Witchcraft
Hoodoo Folk Magic
Moon Magic
Meditation
The Cailleach
Animal Magic
Sun Magic
Triple Goddess

Other Moon Books
The Art of Ritual
Beneath the Moon
Witchcraft … into the Wilds
Grimoire of a Kitchen Witch
A Kitchen Witch's World of Magical Foods
A Kitchen Witch's World of Magical Plants & Herbs
Arc of the Goddess (co-written with Tracey Roberts)
Moon Books Gods & Goddesses Colouring Book (Patterson family)
Practically Pagan: An Alternative Guide to Cooking

Llewellyn
Curative Magic
A Witch for All Seasons: Spells, Rituals, Festivals, and Magic

MOON
BOOKS

PAGANISM & SHAMANISM

What is Paganism? A religion, a spirituality, an alternative belief system, nature worship? You can find support for all these definitions (and many more) in dictionaries, encyclopaedias, and text books of religion, but subscribe to any one and the truth will evade you. Above all Paganism is a creative pursuit, an encounter with reality, an exploration of meaning and an expression of the soul. Druids, Heathens, Wiccans and others, all contribute their insights and literary riches to the Pagan tradition. Moon Books invites you to begin or to deepen your own encounter, right here, right now.

If you have enjoyed this book, why not tell other readers by posting a review on your preferred book site.

Medicine for the Soul
The Complete Book of Shamanic Healing
Ross Heaven
All you will ever need to know about shamanic healing and how to
become your own shaman...
Paperback: 978-1-78099-419-2 ebook: 978-1-78099-420-8

Shaman Pathways – The Druid Shaman
Exploring the Celtic Otherworld
Danu Forest
A practical guide to Celtic shamanism with exercises and
techniques as well as traditional lore for exploring the Celtic
Otherworld.
Paperback: 978-1-78099-615-8 ebook: 978-1-78099-616-5

Traditional Witchcraft for the Woods and Forests
A Witch's Guide to the Woodland with Guided Meditations and
Pathworking
Mélusine Draco
A Witch's guide to walking alone in the woods, with guided
meditations and pathworking.
Paperback: 978-1-84694-803-9 ebook: 978-1-84694-804-6

Wild Earth, Wild Soul
A Manual for an Ecstatic Culture
Bill Pfeiffer
Imagine a nature-based culture so alive and so connected,
spreading like wildfire. This book is the first flame...
Paperback: 978-1-78099-187-0 ebook: 978-1-78099-188-7

Naming the Goddess
Trevor Greenfield
Naming the Goddess is written by over eighty adherents and
scholars of Goddess and Goddess Spirituality.
Paperback: 978-1-78279-476-9 ebook: 978-1-78279-475-2

Shapeshifting into Higher Consciousness
Heal and Transform Yourself and Our World with Ancient
Shamanic and Modern Methods
Llyn Roberts
Ancient and modern methods that you can use every day to
transform yourself and make a positive difference in the world.
Paperback: 978-1-84694-843-5 ebook: 978-1-84694-844-2

Readers of ebooks can buy or view any of these bestsellers by
clicking on the live link in the title. Most titles are published in
paperback and as an ebook. Paperbacks are available in traditional
bookshops. Both print and ebook formats are available online.

Find more titles and sign up to our readers' newsletter at
http://www.johnhuntpublishing.com/paganism
Follow us on Facebook at https://www.facebook.com/MoonBooks
and Twitter at https://twitter.com/MoonBooksJHP